The Velvet Underground Handbook

M. C. Kostek

Black Spring Press

First Published in 1992 by Black Spring Press

FIRST EDITION

Black Spring Press Ltd
63 Harlescott Road
London SE15 3DA

All rights reserved. No part of this publication may be reproduced, stored in or introduced into a retrieval system or transmitted in any form or by any means, electronic, mechanical, photocopying, recording or otherwise, without the prior written permission of the publisher.

Copyright © M. C. Kostek

ISBN 0 948238 12 7

Printed and bound in Great Britain by
The Guernsey Press Co. Ltd., Guernsey, Channel Islands

Contents

Preface	9
Introduction: **'Inevitably Exploding'**	13
Timeline	21

Pre-Velvet Underground
Pre-VU Records Featuring Lou Reed	35
Pre-VU Songs Written by Lou Reed	39

Velvet Underground Discographies
45s and EPs	47
Original LP Releases	57
Unreleased Songs Copywritten by Lou Reed Whilst a Member of the VU	64
VU Compilations	65
VU Tracks on Various Artist Compilations, Radio Shows Etc	75
Records of Related Interest	83

Cover Versions of VU Songs
Recorded VU Covers	88
VU Covers Performed Live	108

Film
VU Films	111
VU Television Appearances	115
Films of Related Interest	119

Print
VU and Related Books	125
VU Related Magazine Articles	147

Appendices
I. The Velvet Underground and Nico – A History of the First Album	171
II. CD Song Order	179
III. Bootlegs	185
IV. Post-VU Solo Discographies (including videos)	213

To Kate and MC3,
for waiting for their particular man

Preface

This was a difficult book to compile. The long task of piecing together the trail of VU-related material issued since 1957 by record companies (some active, most not), clubs, publishers, photographers, and fans around the world was formidable. Another challenge was how to overcome the difficulties of indexing, formatting, and standardizing, so as to explain as much as possible of the VU mystery. There is great romance in the unknown – you can fill in the blanks to your own liking; this is especially true in Europe, where the band is perhaps best appreciated, but where accurate information is hard to come by. The legend of the VU/Warhol/EPI/Factory/Reed/Cale/Nico et al. axis grows with each CD retrospective, each museum tribute, and ultimately I feel there is so much misinformation around that it interferes with our appreciation of the music. The band's accomplishments can stand the light of day, and it's such light which the present volume hopes to shed.

Little was known at the time about the original albums and singles as they were released, never mind all the subsequent films, compilation records, and books made available after the band's break-up.

The goal of this book is to allow people to know more about the band and the music they made. For casual fans, there is all the basic information about the records and major events in the band's life. For collectors, there are complete listings for singles, EPs, reissues, et al., as well as a history of the first album. I've included all information and references to the band from the beginning to 1972, and the significant listings since. I've included information about Angus MacLise (their first drummer) and others from that time such as Tony Conrad, Piero Heliczer and LaMonte Young because they had much to do with the beginnings of the Velvet Underground; and besides, that entire era is neglected and deserves attention. The Velvet Underground stand at the apex of a rich load of interesting, challenging, exciting art.

I have tried to make this book as accurate as possible. When I was in doubt about something, I left it out. If you can fill in a space, or have additions, corrections, or criticisms, please write me care of the Velvet Underground Appreciation Society, 5721 SE Laguna Avenue, Stuart FL 34997-7828 USA. (The VUAS is a small endeavor run by myself along with my wife Kate. We try to collect and catalog all information related to the VU, both past and present, and we publish a magazine, 'What Goes On', of VU history, reviews, photographs. Anyone interested in trading or selling tapes, records, photographs, posters – anything at all related to the VU – should please contact us.)

Many thanks belong here. Thanks to Kate and MC3, and our parents, for all their time and support, to Phil 'Felipe' Milstein, who begat this in 1978, and, for their invaluable help and kindness in sharing their time and collections with me: Harry and Riet Waanders, Ignacio y Lola Julia, Dom Molumby, Jim Flynn Curtin, Bill Allerton, Miles Gore, Hias Schaschko, Judith Schnaubelt, Ivo Zazvorka, Carsten & Jutta Brandt, Jay Reeg, Chris Carter, Arie Houtman, Eric Lord, Richard Bean and Sterling Morrison.

The following abbreviations have been used:

w/	with	gtr	guitar
b/w	backed with	vcl	vocal
PS	picture sleeve	dms	drums
45	45rpm single	kbds	keyboards
v.a.	various artists	b&w	black and white
E.P.I.	Andy Warhol's Exploding Plastic Inevitable		

M. C. Kostek

Introduction
Inevitably Exploding

Think about the rock and roll music of the 1960s. What comes to mind? Mad scenes whirling around the Beatles, the Rolling Stones, and Bob Dylan? Indeed, they were the giants then, and they made music that is still potent today, with a lot more to offer than most that's come along since. Those were unusual times. Wild bands such as the Who, Jefferson Airplane, the Yardbirds, the 13th Floor Elevators were actually having Top 40 hits. Folk-rock, hippie psychedelia, r&b, garage, blues, all flowed together in one unique, wide-open time.

However, one band in the mid-60s had little to do with the hippie scene, never got played on commercial radio, never played the Fillmore East or Woodstock, played the Fillmore West only once, never truly toured Europe, was never profiled in Rolling Stone, never sold many records in the five short years they were together. Despite all this, the Velvet Underground has emerged, twenty-five years after their first album was released, as a band as important as the Beatles, Dylan, or the Stones in terms of having made lasting music and influencing the cause of rock and roll.

Brian Eno's quip about how not many people bought **The Velvet Underground & Nico** album but of those who did, every one went out and formed a band carries much truth. Many of the most creative people in rock music from the 70s – the Stooges, New York Dolls, Patti Smith, Television, Pere Ubu, Ramones, Richard Hell,

Jonathan Richman, Roxy Music, David Bowie, Buzzcocks, Talking Heads, Wire, Cabaret Voltaire, and yes, Brian Eno – the 80s – Joy Division, REM, Laurie Anderson, Magazine, The Smiths, Nick Cave, Throbbing Gristle and Psychic TV, Public Image Ltd, Swans, Sonic Youth, The Fall, The Jesus & Mary Chain, UT, Cowboy Junkies, Hugo Largo, and on and on into the 90s – strongly reflect and validate the Velvets' massive musical influence.

In Czechoslovakia, **White Light/White Heat** was a rallying point, a galvanizing example of freedom of expression for those pushing for freedom in the 60s, and again in the 80s, and people were imprisoned for years for playing VU songs, for having a VU tape or printed lyrics. (In Prague today, the Velvet Revival Band keeps this defiant spirit alive by playing only VU songs.) And last November 17th, Czechoslovakia's independence day, President Havel (the man who brought a tape of **White Light/White Heat** back from New York in 1968 and a decade later led the 'Velvet Revolution') and Radio One in Prague held a celebration. Who did they invite? – The Velvet Underground.

Over 800 bands have now done cover versions of Velvet Underground songs (see later listing for the more interesting ones), and there's an unending tape trail of new bands doing versions today. Twenty years after the VU ended, young bands from all around the world, from Australia, Japan, Canada, Finland, Spain, cite the VU as a major influence. **Rolling Stone**'s 1987 'Critic's Poll' placed three of the first four VU LPs in the 'Top 100 LPs of the Last 20 Years'; the banana LP topped off at number 21, **Loaded** at 32 and the third LP at 97. And that from a periodical which feuded with the band while they were together: **Rolling Stone** never wrote a feature on the VU, and never even reviewed the **VU & Nico** or **White Light** until they were re-issued in 1985. (The band have often had a higher reputation in Europe than in their home country, and in 1988 the readers of **New Musical Express** voted the **VU & Nico** the fifth best album of all time.)

In England, a 5-record box set retrospective with a

limited edition of 10,000 recently sold out so quickly that another 10,000 were made – fifteen years after the band broke up. In Australia, national radio shows have been given over to recalling the history of the band and interviews with the members. A complete, three-CD retrospective is planned there for 1992. Authoritative TV specials on the band have been made in England and Spain, and now the entire VU catalog is available again in the USA (on LP, cassette and CD), and selling better today than when the band was together. And on the 15th June 1990 the Foundation Cartier outside of Paris held a lush Warhol-VU show, making headlines as the band reunited for one song; an expensive French 4 CD box set reissue edition of 5,000 commemorating the show disappeared so fast it never even made it to England. And in Hamburg, Germany, two young people, working with a tiny budget, put together a modest museum show and attracted 30,000 visitors in three months. And two not-quite-as-young people working with an even smaller budget (ok, ok, my wife and I) spend too much time compiling information and rarities on this band for a fanzine whose fourth issue sells over 5,000 copies in 3 weeks. How is this possible? Ten new VU bootlegs have appeared in 1991. Why do so many people still take this band seriously today? Even the Rock & Roll Hall of Fame beckons: the Velvets were nominated in their first year of eligibility.

In effect, the VU were Andy Warhol's house band. Their stance was one of playing what they wanted to play, doing what they wanted to do – hey! sounds-of-the-60s ethics – they weren't so far from their times after all. They never made a record with the idea of selling it (**Loaded** excepted, perhaps). Members of the band have gone on to distinguished, exciting solo careers, largely continuing the non-compromising VU tradition. All this activity is a quiet, hep thing. It's still cool to like the VU. They can hardly be co-opted: they never get shown on MTV. Even if Kurt Loder wanted to show them, there's hardly any footage available. (A few years back, Ben Edmunds had finished compiling Doors' footage for a video release, and began working on a Velvet Underground set. He had to stop after a few months – there's almost nothing to be found, and most of what there is on film just has the band blasting out improvised noise.) 60s retro collections rarely, if ever, carry a VU track. Their amps won't wind up on Southeby's block, and there are no gold records to decorate Hard Rock Cafes around the globe. PolyGram has released nothing new from the band since 1974 except the collections of out-takes **V.U.** and **Another View**, and the record company and band fought bitterly about these. (They also fought bitterly over the other posthumous releases of **Live at Max's** and **Live 1969**.) The VU did much to fight off success, even beyond writing songs about heroin and S&M: they fought with the poobah kingmakers of the 60s (Bill Graham, Jann Wenner, and eventually, Andy Warhol). They rebuffed Brian Epstein when he was interested in working with them. The VU's anti-stance runs much deeper and truer than that thrown up by the punk rebels of the 70s; for the VU it wasn't just a stance.

Of course the original VU/EPI center could never hold. It's amazing that these people, who were all more stubborn than each other, stayed together for so long. As the band's members drifted away, or were driven away, the resultant albums reflect the layers being exposed. Yes, they have a style that grates, but so much more. The first album is brimming with a world of ideas, depth, talent, nerve – Nico's beautiful, fragile, tough/cool as she sings Lou's wonderful songs of love and betrayal. (They made her sing **Femme Fatale** over and over again until, exhausted, she attained just the right tone of utter resignation they were looking for.) John Cale can play a beautiful melody, or a firestorm. He can caress, he can pound with the best, with barely-controlled passion. Along with Nico's other-world voice, he gave the band technique, punch and fire no other band has ever had. The unceasing piano of **All Tomorrow's Parties**, the bass wallop of **European Son**, the eerie viola propulsion in **Heroin**, the exotic, beautiful atmospheres of **The Black Angel's Death Song** and **Venus In Furs**, all this Cale brought to the band. He knew how to play, how to repeat for effect, how to take the listener to places he'd never been before. And he was part of the band: listen to the perfect intro. to **I'm Waiting For The Man**: in ten seconds we're on the street, hearing this band play perfectly, making that absolutely identifiable Velvet Underground sound. The power that blew them apart also fueled their music.

White Light/White Heat was made after the early days were long over. Gone were Andy, the EPI, and Nico. The competition/comradeship that brought them all together had frayed badly for the four still remaining. **White Light** is a sonic war. There's none of Nico's grace and mystery. **Here She Comes Now** was written for her to sing, and while she did sing it live, she was long gone when the time came to record it. Imagine the song with her vocals. But the band's power is in evidence with the frenzied, unequaled bass of **White Light**, with Lou's frenetic guitar on **I Heard Her Call My Name**, and it culminates in the one-take-only war that was **Sister Ray**. Lou could whip the 12-string into a blur and squeeze out noises from the netherlands while singing new lyrics as he went along; Sterling is a perfect compliment, with taste and chops, always conscious of the song, of sustaining the structure, while also roaming far and wide: Moe proves her solid worth just by keeping up with them.

The third album, **The Velvet Underground**, shows how great a unit Lou, Sterling and Moe had become, and how well Doug could compliment them. There is none of Cale's force and style here, so it's up to the band to sing and play the songs in a straightahead fashion, and Lou and Sterling do just that. Sparse, lean guitars, perfect simplicity. They quietly cook **What Goes On** until the knowledge of what a fine song this is sneaks up on the listener – it feels like this groove should go on forever. Songs that were originally overlooked, such as **I'm Set Free** and **Beginning To See The Light**, shine brightly in the clear sound of the CD. This is a fine album, one that most everyone missed when it came out. Great songs by Lou, wonderfully played by the Velvet Underground.

Loaded is the final round for the VU. Doug is too much in the recording, keeping it too light, too fluid. It sounds too much like a rock and roll record. The others were too busy or sick to work on it much, and it's largely Doug in evidence here. A fine record, it nonetheless shows how much Lou, Sterling and Moe meant to the Velvet Underground.

The scope and verve of the Velvet Underground are summed up well by their first releases. In 1966, before the first album came out, they released two singles. Verve released a 45 with a picture sleeve of **All Tomorrow's Parties** b/w **I'll Be Your Mirror**. While at the same time, the very arty (published in a box, with posters, cut-outs, etc.) magazine **Aspen** did a 'Pop' issue – Warhol was guest editor – and one of the items in the box was a flexi-disc by the VU called **Loop** – six minutes of screeching, repetitive bass guitar feedback. Two records: the fragile yet powerful beauty of Nico singing Reed's **All Tomorrow's Parties** and the boundless noise of **Loop**. The rock/pop world had never heard such sounds, and never such range from one band. It was clear from the start that this band was going places Dylan, the Beatles and the Stones never dared to explore.

For all the overly-simplified comparisons between the New York mean streets/hard drugs scene of the VU versus the West Coast hippie/soft drugs haze, there are important factors to remember when thinking about this time in the mid-1960s. The important point about the 1960s is that this was a time when everything was being reconsidered, reevaluated. People were changing their values, their clothes, their life-styles. Everything was open: the way they shook hands, accumulated or shed possessions, raised children, and the music they listened to. The VU operated in this open air of change, and pushed themselves to make the music they wanted, without compromise. Think of the immediate peer group the band had: their first audiences were the people going to see the wildest films in New York in 1965, the directors of which, such as Piero Heliczer, Jonas Mekas and Jack Smith, lived for experimentation. And then there was

Andy Warhol and the Factory crowd, who wanted fabulous new kicks, fabulous open minds, every day. These were not kids in Liverpool's Cavern or Hamburg's rock clubs, yelling for the band to rock harder and 'make show.' The Falling Spikes (as one early form of the band was known) had no folk or blues heritage to be true to. Another important factor was that the money-making music machine was not yet in place. Rock music in 1966 was still new; it had provided some hits in the 1950s and more were emerging, but a major label could sign a band such as the Velvet Underground and generally leave them alone to make the music they wanted. The label bosses didn't know what to do with it when they got it, but at least the records got made. There was no tested formula then for making money; to these record companies, the world was flying apart when animals such as the Beatles, Stones, Dylan and the Animals could have hit records. So they kept their hands off.

The Velvet Underground was a happy accident. They had talent obvious enough to attract Warhol, Epstein, Atlantic's Ahmet Ertegun, producer Tom Wilson, talent clear enough to be signed to two major labels. They were a once-in-a-lifetime combination. Look at this line-up: Lou Reed took the best r&b and doo-wop of the 50s and mixed it with the garage punk stomp of the early 60s, while honing his writing skills at Syracuse University, studying Latin poetry and Greek drama, and, for a world-class course in talent, paranoia and genius, being taught by Delmore Schwartz. Further, he learnt songwriting craft at a low-budget Tin Pan Alley sweat shop, Pickwick Records. Meeting Sterling Morrison, the two discovered much in common: a fondness for Bo Diddley's absolute primal beat, wild r&b records, and open-minded intelligence. Angus MacLise fueled the level of experimentation and their willingness to move beyond regular r&b. Moe Tucker added a necessary anchor both with her percussion and her personality. They were all fiercely proud of what they were doing and would brook no compromise. They were the first rock band on a major label who made no compromises for commercial success. They would make it on their terms or not at all.

John Cale brought a knowledge of the European classics and of the new music of the day: he was familiar with Xenakis, Stockhausen, Copeland and Satie. Adding his eerie drones and avant garde screech, inspired by John Cage and LaMonte Young, fabulously complemented the VU's hard-boiled songs of 60s street life, of drugs, love, S&M, paranoia.

Heroin, the band's trademark song, is about heroin, but also so much more. The vicarious experience Lou provides for us in that song works because it gives us an idea of the entire experience; it is also a metaphor which he uses to explore the idea of how to deal with the world when it has become too much for us. The Velvet Underground is itself a "great big clipper ship taking us from this here land to that". It's a fine tour that works on many levels. Lou's tales of the Factory crowd work as fairy stories told of wonderful and awful characters, as tales which are also explorations into all of our lives. And the passion and power in the music behind these lyrics sets them apart, and gives the songs their lasting quality. Add Warhol's knack for outrageous/courageous marketing, and Nico's incomparable style, and you have an event, a singular combination of many cultures and styles: European, avant-garde, Wagnerian opera, North American r&b and doo-wop, Eastern mysticism, all blended in the mixer of mid-60s openness. Artistic values from all these cultures met crass Tin Pan Alley commerce and the anti-commerce of underground filmmaking. This was a unique burst of culture, fueled by an open atmosphere of creativity. The period may be over, but its inspiration flows on.

Timeline

The members of the Velvet Underground went from selling blood and posing as murderers for exploitation magazines in order to pay the rent to being commissioned by the Brooklyn Academy of Music to write a requiem for the life of America's artist of the century, their patron, Andy Warhol.

Nico was born in the late 30s in Cologne, Germany, but all the other members were born in the 40s – Lou in Brooklyn, Moe, original drummer Angus MacLise and Sterling on Long Island; John Cale was born in Wales. Favorites emerged early in their music listening: Nico recalled her mother taking her to the opera; Cale was a child prodigy in classical music, and developed an early interest in electronic and avant-garde music; Lou's life was figuratively saved by the excitement coming from his radio: New York doo-wop and r&b (he recalls learning rhythm guitar from James Brown records); Sterling had similar tastes – Bo Diddley records augmented his trumpet lessons; Moe bashed along in her room to Chuck Berry, Ricky Nelson and Beatles records; Angus listened to Asian music along with his childhood friend Piero Heliczer.

1957... **Lou** is part of several teen combos. One, called the **Jades**, change their name to the **Shades** when it's time to record a single and they learn there are many other 'Jades' already in the world.

1959... **Nico** has been modeling around Europe and

visits the set of **La Dolce Vita**. Director **Federico Fellini** is impressed enough by her presence to create a part in the film for her.

1962... **Nico** continues modeling and has a part in a French B-movie, **Sweet Skin**.

1963... **Lou** is attending **Syracuse University** in upstate New York and meets **Sterling Morrison**: Sterling is initially attracted by the blasts of guitar coming out of Lou's dorm window.

John Cale wins a **Leonard Bernstein Scholarship** to attend **Tanglewood Conservatory** in western Massachusetts, about 125 miles from New York. He later moves to New York and begins working with **Tony Conrad** and **Marion Zazeela** in **LaMonte Young's Dream Syndicate**.

1964... **Lou** is graduated from Syracuse (after some drug escapades) and moves to New York City after landing a job with **Pickwick Records** as a staff songwriter. Pickwick specialize in issuing budget-line records: they license old material by artists with current hits, and they also release their own records of 'soundalike' material. Lou is part of the writing/recording team that produces surf songs, 'Motown' songs, 'Beatles' songs, whatever is hot.

Lou meets **John Cale** at a party and later shows him some of his songs: **Heroin**, **Venus In Furs**. John is impressed by these bold songs that flow against the current pop/folk trends; they begin to work together.

Pickwick chooses one of Lou's songs, **The Ostrich**, to release as a single, and put together a group to be known as **The Primitives** to play live to push it: **Cale**, **Tony Conrad** and **Walter DeMaria** join **Lou** as the live Primitives for a few shows before the 45 fades.

Lou and **John** settle down in Manhattan to work out some musical ideas.

1965... **John** and **Lou** meet **Angus MacLise**, and **Lou** meets **Sterling** again. They all move into low low rent flats on the lower East Side of Manhattan. **Lou** and **John** sell blood, sing on street corners, and pose as mass murder/rapist/incest types for a **Police Gazette**-style magazine to get money to live. **Lou**, **John**, **Sterling** and **Angus** practice songs and jam together.

Angus introduces the group to his friend **Piero Heliczer**, who has been making experimental films. He invites the band, known under many names such as the **Warlocks** and **Falling Spikes**, to provide the music at screenings of his films and of those by other directors such as **Jonas Mekas** and **Jack Smith**. They decide on their name when **Tony Conrad** finds a paperback book on the sidewalk: **The Velvet Underground** is the title of an exploitative, pseudo-scientific 'study' about wife-swapping in suburbia and other signs of the new immorality.

Lou and **John** make their own tapes of noise and frolic. In the winter the four make a demo tape and send it off to several contacts in the USA and UK (including **Miles Copeland**, who will one day head IRS Records).

In the UK **Nico** meets **Jimmy Page**, who helps her record a 45 for **Rolling Stones** manager **Andrew Oldham's** label **Immediate**.

Back in the states, **Angus** leaves the **VU** rather than compromise his principles and accept money for his art at their first paid ($75) gig, 11 December 1965, at a high school in New Jersey. **Jim Tucker**, a mutual friend of Sterling and Lou's, suggests his sister **Maureen** to replace Angus. 'Moe' is a drummer, and what's more has an amplifier. **Moe** auditions and her straight-beat African-rooted style works for the others.

The band gets a residency at a Greenwich Village spot named the **Cafe Bizarre**. **Brigid Polk** sees them there and later returns with her friend, **Andy Warhol**. Andy is struck by the band and asks them to work with him on a new project of his: a bombardment of sound, light, film and dance.

1966... In January Andy is featured on the Public Broadcasting's TV show **American Artists**. He introduces the VU, who blast home **Heroin** and **Venus In Furs**. Andy later introduces the band to **Nico**, who has arrived in New York and been 'discovered' by Andy.

John, Moe, Lou, Sterling; probably 1966

Warhol suggests that it would be very glamorous for this stunning, eerie beauty to sing a few songs, and the band go along with the idea. They find a place large enough to hold Andy's happening project: the Polish National Home, known as the **Dom** (Polish for 'home'), is in a very untrendy part of Greenwich Village, with a low rent and good home cooking.

The **Factory**, Warhol's studio, becomes home base for the VU, and they become part of the daily parade of characters and excitement. They rehearse there, hang out there, and wait to choose which party invitations they will accept so they can eat. Warhol puts up enough money for them to record an album. They lay down basic tracks in New York at a makeshift studio. **Tom Wilson**, a talented producer for **Columbia**, hears them live and is intrigued. Wilson has not only produced talents such as **Bob Dylan** with care and craft, but he has also produced hits for **Simon & Garfunkel** and the **Animals**. He is leaving Columbia for a house-producer job at **MGM Records**, and tells Andy and the VU he'll get them a deal there. The tracks the VU cut in New York are very rough, very basic, and Wilson brings the band to **Los Angeles** to do some polishing. Andy visits local record shops to see what album cover designs work: he finds that white covers are the most striking, and that less is more in terms of print. All agree on the banana cover and the record is ready to go.

Andy's mass happening, the **Exploding Plastic Inevitable**, hits the Dom in New York City like a bomb. The EPI is, at very least, the first rock and roll light show. But more than this, it is blasting music/noise, several films shown at the same time on the wall, strobe lights flashing everywhere, dancers careering with whips – a sensory overload. The Dom becomes *the* place to be. The EPI hits the road: northeast, midwest, California. Much bad press from middle-class art critics still holding a grudge over Andy's soup cans; this EPI abomination is way over the top. A trendy L.A. scenemaker at the time, **Cher**, comments: "The only thing it will replace is suicide". While in **San Francisco**, the VU play the Fillmore West and fight with **Bill Graham**, thus making an enemy of the most important promoter in rock.

In the second half of 1966 the VU's first recordings are released: **Noise** and the 45s of **All Tomorrow's Parties/I'll Be Your Mirror** and **Sunday Morning/Femme Fatale**. In November the band play at an outdoor wedding ceremony in Detroit, publicised as the nation's first 'Mod Wedding' and part of a three-day 'Carnaby Street Fun Festival'. The December issue of **Aspen Magazine** features a flexi-disc of one of those experimental tapes John had made: a six-minute recording of slowly rising and falling bass and feedback roar named **Loop**.

1967... In March, after nearly a year's delay, MGM release **The Velvet Underground & Nico** album on what had been their jazz label, **Verve**. Shortly after the LP is released one of the Warhol entourage, **Eric Emerson**, is arrested on a drug charge. Desperate for money, he sues MGM for using his photograph on the album cover without his permission – he appears upside-down, as part of the EPI montage, on the back cover. Verve halt production and promotion of the album while they put stickers over the photograph, air-brushing Emerson out of the picture on future editions. Valuable time and impetus is lost. **Nico leaves** the band in the spring, the uneasy association ending

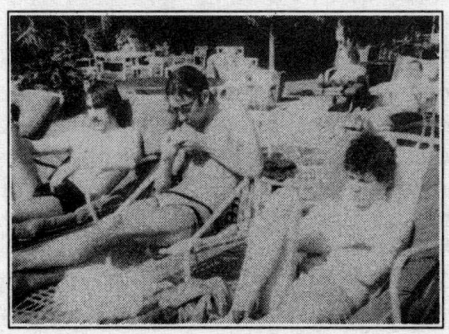

Sterling, John, Lou; probably in Los Angeles, 1967

23

when she is rebuffed in her desire to sing more of the songs, including **Heroin**. Andy also leaves, tiring of the EPI scene. (On **Songs For Drella**, Lou Reed sings that he fired Andy, after Andy called the band dilettantes for playing so many art museums and not more clubs.)

The band have also become alienated from their home town. They returned from their California trip in 1966 to find their home, the Dom, taken from them by underhand promoters. New York City radio, known as the most conservative radio in the USA, relative to its location, is giving them scant airplay. With other suitable places to play hard to find in New York, the VU adopt Boston as their home. The **Boston Tea Party**, an old church, is a great place to play, with appreciative audiences, and their manager, **Steve Sesnick**, gets them Tea Party gigs early and often as he is part owner of the club. (They will not play again in New York City until the spring of 1970.)

Lou at Disneyland, 1967

Lou, Sterling and John build an odd relationship. Competition fuels it – competition for women, drugs, solos, everything – and gives the band its curious power, but it also makes for many lingering feuds. When it comes to recording the second album they cannot agree on how to play a particular new, long song. Eventually they agree on just the beginning and the ending, and that there will be only one take, with no overdubs. They load in all their effects boxes and blasting equipment, and begin. All four crank up, trying to blow the others out of the room. John has the most sonic boosters, and it is his keyboard solo that finally emerges from the din half-way through **Sister Ray**.

1968... **White Light/ White Heat** is released in January. The black-on-black cover was a suggestion of Andy's, and a photograph of **Joe Dellasandro**'s tattooed arm lends it a sleek menace.

An MGM promo shot for White Light/White Heat, 1967

None of the singles from the first album received much attention, and now **White Light/White Heat** backed with **Here She Comes Now** gets even less. The white noise roar of the album delights EPI fans but disgusts most other listeners. (There was little precedent in popular music for the first VU album, and so too with **White Light/ White Heat**. Even the other 'bad boys' of rock, such as **The Rolling Stones** and **The Animals**,

Live at The Boston Tea Party, 1968

didn't make records like this; the shocking feedback bursts used by **The Who** were brief and very occasional. **Kick Out The Jams** was a year away, **The Stooges** three years away, **Metal Machine Music** nine, and **Never Mind The Bollocks** twelve.) The band continues to tour coast to coast, having asked MGM to put promotional money into tour support rather than pushing the LP. The live shows are notable in that they allow for much improvisation, especially in **Sister Ray**, which is different most every night. Also, Lou has a knack of improvising new lyrics and personae on the spot. Every night is an adventure.

John Cale

4th June, 1968 – **Valerie Solanas** enters the Factory with a gun and shoots Warhol, wounding him seriously.

One night in **September**, Lou calls Moe and Sterling to a pub in New York City. There he announces that **John is out of the band**; the unending competition has become too much for Lou to handle. Moe and Sterling regretfully side with Lou in this; after all, he is the main singer/songwriter. For a replacement they select **Doug Yule**, a young bassist/keyboard player they know from Boston. Doug can play in the same general style as John, though without the manic creativity. He can also sing, and, most importantly, he seems to pose none of the threat, creative or otherwise, that John represented. Doug fits in well enough for the VU to remain a potent live band (**Live 1969** is made with Doug). They continue to tour but record sales are slow. Work is begun on the third album, **The Velvet Underground**, in the fall, but before the band arrive at the studio in Los Angeles they find that most of their equipment,

Lou Reed, November 1968

26

including most of the sonic boom boxes used on the last album, has been stolen at the airport. They proceed with recording anyway, choosing to record very simply, quietly.

1969... **The Velvet Underground** is released in March. Coming at the height of the psychedelic age, the album is a direct contrast not only to the production and experimentation values that had become standard since **Sgt. Pepper**, but also a complete reversal from the **White Light** white roar. Adding to the confusion is the lack of credits on the cover. The final blow to any chance of success for the album is the mix. MGM's house producer, **Val Valentin**, had done a clear, fine-sounding mix (as heard on the 1985 reissue). Lou, however, wanted his own mix – a very muffled, claustrophobic one, with almost no bass and all tones dampened. The band had never played nor sung so well, so clearly, and perversely Lou obscures that fact with the mix. The effect is unique; the record sounds as if it's coming from the next room, which makes it a great mood piece but is not good for sales.

Moe, November 1968

A promo shot of the band, Los Angeles, November 1968

1970... MGM give up after the third album. **Atlantic** sign the band to a two-record deal and in the spring work

27

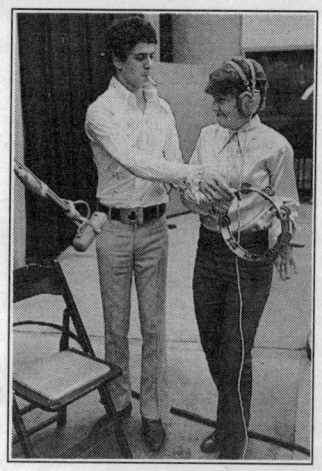

Recording the third album...

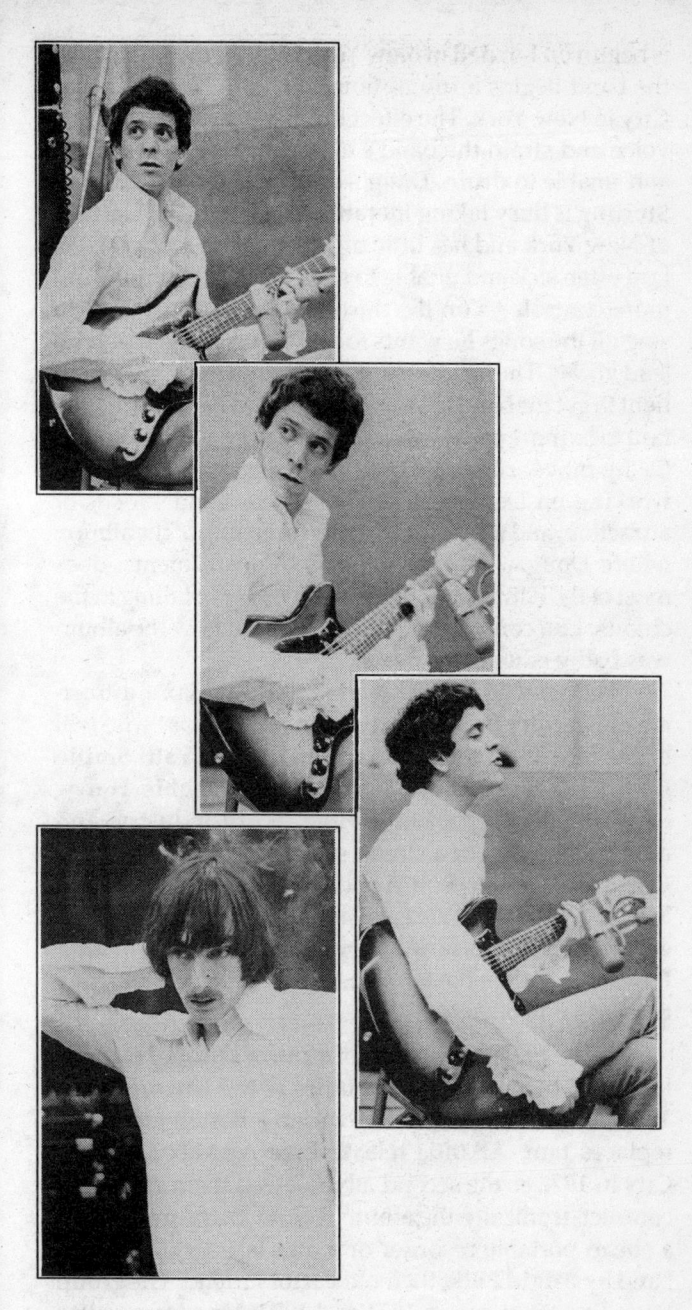

...in Los Angeles, 1968/69

is begun on **Loaded** in New York City. At the same time, the band begins a run as house band at **Max's Kansas City** in New York. The effect this has is to exhaust Lou's voice and strain the band's energies. **Moe** is pregnant, and unable to drum. Doug's brother **Billy Yule** fills in. **Sterling** is busy taking literature classes at **City College of New York** and has little time to gig and record. With Lou often sick and unable to sing, Doug takes more and more control. As on the third album, Lou is unable to sing all the songs he wants to and Doug is given several lead vocals. The band's manager, **Steve Sesnick**, is impatient to get the band to the next level, and has been urging Lou to be more of a showman on stage. Lou does do more flashy moves on stage, but not enough. Sesnick begins working on Doug to take over as the band's focus of attraction, and this extends to the recording of the album, where Doug winds up playing six instruments, does most of the editing and mixing, and gets top billing in the credits. Lou complains to this day about how the album was badly edited and mixed.

The band goes down a great storm at Max's, attracting old Factory friends as well as many of those who will be the movers in the 1970s, eg **Jim Carroll**, **Patti Smith**, **David Johansen**, **Tom Verlaine** and **Debbie Harry**. However, feeling beaten by the record industry, and now a man without a strong support band behind him, **Lou quits** the band on **August 23**, after an evening at Max's. **Loaded** is released in September, but no hits emerge. The band, now led by Doug, carries on. **Walter Powers**, another Boston musician, replaces Lou. **Moe returns** on drums.

1971 – 1973... On the eve of a tour of Europe, **Sterling leaves** to begin literature studies at the **University of Texas at Austin**. **Willie Alexander**, a Boston mainstay, replaces him. Atlantic release **Live At Max's Kansas City** in 1972 as the second album owed them under the contract. Ironically the album is from a tape made with a cheap portable recorder on Lou's last night with the band by **Brigid Polk**, their old Factory friend. The group tours Europe twice, in 1971 and 1972. **Moe leaves** after the second trip. **Doug** records what is essentially a solo album, **Squeeze**, in London in 1972 under the VU name, with Deep Purple's drummer **Ian Paice** the only other musician on the record. In mid-1973 Doug gives up the VU ghost.

15 June, 1990... At an Andy Warhol/Velvet Underground exhibition in the grounds of the Foundation Cartier outside Paris, France, John, Lou, Sterling and Moe **reform** the Velvet Underground for one song. They play **Heroin**, and thank Andy.

To the present...

John Cale has gone on to record fifteen solo albums since 1970, and has collaborated with many other musicians, including **Terry Riley**, **Brian Eno** and **Lou Reed**. He has done production work for **Nico**, **The Stooges**, **Patti Smith**, **The Modern Lovers**, **Squeeze**, **Ian Hunter**, and many others. He has worked as sideman for **Eno**, **Ian Hunter**, **Nick Drake**, **Mike Heron**, **William Burroughs**, and many others, and has contributed music to several films and been commissioned by the government of Holland to set some **Dylan Thomas** poetry to music (**The Falklands Suite**). He is currently working on a musical piece with **Bob Neuwirth** (**The Last Day On Earth**), another atmospheric mood piece (**Sanctus**), and has recently released a new album, **Paris S'Eveille**. Rhino Records is planning a 2-CD retrospective for later in 1992. He currently lives in New York City.

Sterling Morrison completed his studies at Austin to receive his **Ph.D. in Medieval Literature** in 1986. He has done little in music since the Velvet days, except to be in a version of the **Bizarros** in Austin in the late 70s, and has done no recording save for Moe Tucker's **I Spent A Week There The Other Night** album. He currently works as a tugboat pilot in Houston, Texas, but toured Europe with Moe in February 1992.

Nico went on to a solo music career distinguished by a complete disregard for musical fashions or trends.

She made nine solo albums, including **Chelsea Girl** (which features **Lou Reed**, **John Cale**, and several collaborative songs which the VU had performed), **The Marble Index**, **The End**, and **Drama of Exile**. She often collaborated with other musicians, including **Bauhaus**, **Marc Almond**, **Neuronium**, and **Kevin Ayers**. She acted in several films by **Philippe Garrel** and others. Nico **died** from a brain hemorrhage **18 July 1988** on the island of Ibiza, off the coast of Spain, after falling from her bicycle.

Lou Reed has continued recording and performing. He has released nineteen albums and contributed music to and acted in several films. He has supported many benefit causes, including **Rock For Amnesty**, **Farm Aid**, **Hurricane Irene**, **Greenpeace** and **Voices of Sun City**. Musical collaborations include work with **David Bowie**, **U2**, **Ruben Blades**, **Nils Lofgren**, **Simple Minds**, and **Kiss**. His selected lyrics were published in 1991 under the title **Between Thought and Expression**; a 3-CD retrospective was released under the same title in 1992. He currently lives in New York City and New Jersey.

Maureen Tucker left the music scene in 1972 to raise five children in Phoenix, Arizona. She played again in the late 70s with a local band, **Paris 1942**, and has gone on to release three solo albums and two EPs. She has done side work with **Lou Reed** and **Sonic Youth**, and lives in Douglas, Georgia.

Moe Tucker in 1982, for the cover of her first solo LP Playin' Possum

Doug Yule worked with Lou Reed on **Sally Can't Dance**, did a tour with Lou in 1975, and later joined **American Flyer** for two albums in 1976-77. Since that time he has worked as an architectural wood-worker in Brooklyn, New York.

Pre-Velvet Underground

Pre-Velvet Underground Records Featuring Lou Reed

The Shades: Leave Her For Me (Lewis Reed) (2:13)/So Blue (Phil Harris-Lewis Reed) (2:08)
Release date: 28 November 1958
Catalog number: Time 1002 (USA 45) mono (deleted)
Musicians: Lou Reed (gtr), Phil Harris (gtr, vocal), King Curtis (sax) (?), plus studio musicians
Producer: not known
Recording dates: 1958
Cover credit: no cover
Of note: The Jades/Shades were Lou's first band.

The Primitives: The Ostrich (Reed-Sims-Vance-Phillips) (2:25)/Sneaky Pete (Reed-Sims-Vance-Phillips) (2:08)
Release date: 1964
Catalog number: Pickwick City PC-1001 (USA 45) mono (deleted)
Musicians: Lou Reed (gtr), plus studio musicians
Producer: L.H.
Recording dates: 1964
Cover credit: no cover
Of note: 1. This 45 from Pickwick studio musicians led to the formation of a live Primitives band that included John Cale.
2. Co-writer Jerry Vance's real name is Jerry Pellegrino.
3. Co-writer Jimmie Sims' real name is Jim Smith.
4. Co-writer Terry Phillips' real name is Philip Teitelbaum; he subsequently worked as a staff producer at Decca.

Ronnie Dove/Terry Philips/Swingin' Teen Sounds Of
Release date: 1965
Catalog number: Design DLP 186 (USA LP) mono (deleted)
Side 1/Ronnie Dove: I'll Be Around (not known), No Greater Love (not known). Terry Philips: This Rose (Sims-Vance-Philips-Reed), Flowers For The Lady (Irby-Philips-Vance-Reed-Sims), This I Promise You (Guiffre-Philips-Sims-Vance). *Side 2*/Ronnie Dove: Saddest Song Of The Year (not known), Party Doll (not known), Wild One (Reed-Philips-Vance-Sims), Everybody's Sweetheart (Baron-Philips-Irby), You (Philips-Vance-Sims)
Musicians: Lou Reed (?), plus studio musicians
Producer: not known
Recording dates: 1964, '65
Cover credit: not known
Of note: It is likely Reed appears on these sessions, especially on the songs he co-authored.

Various Artists/Soundsville!
Release date: 1965
Catalog number: Design DLP 187 (USA LP) mono, SDLP 187 stereo (deleted)
Side 1/Don't Turn My World Upside Down (all songs written by Reed-Philips-Vance-Sims, except 7), Soul City, Teardrop In The Sand, Wonderful World of Love, You're Driving Me Insane. *Side 2*/First Impression, I'm Gonna Fight, I've Got A Tiger In My Tank (Reed-Philips-Vance-Sims-Motta), Cycle Annie, Johnny Won't Surf No More, It's Hard For A Girl In A World Full Of Men
Musicians: Lou Reed (gtr, vcl on 5, 9; probably gtr, backing vocals on the rest), plus studio musicians
Producer: not known
Recording dates: 1964, '65
Cover credit: not known
Of note: The 'stereo' edition is in 'AuthentiPhonic Stereo Process', which is Pickwick's way of telling you they added some echo to the original mono tapes.

The Intimates: I've Got A Tiger In My Tank (Motta-Philips-Reed-Sims-Vance) (2:09)/Smart Too Late (Soloway-Glaser)
Release date: 1965(?)
Catalog number: Epic 5-9743 (USA 45) mono (deleted)
Musicians: not known
Musical Director: Jerry Vance
Producer: ALH
Recording dates: 1965 (?)
Cover credit: not known
Of note: 1. Same track as the **Soundsville!** version, with added 'tiger' roars.
2. Epic leased this from Pickwick and probably released it only as a promo to see if it would get radio play as a novelty hit.

Robertha Williams: Tell Mama Not To Cry (Philips-Reed-Sims-Vance)/Maybe Tomorrow (Philips-Vance-Sims-Reed)
Release date: 1965
Catalog number: Uptown 707 (USA 45) mono (deleted)
Musicians: not known
Producer: not known
Recording dates: 1965 (?)
Cover credit: not known
Of note: Uptown was a Pickwick sub-label.

Irma Thomas/Maxine Brown/Ronnie Dickerson
Release date: 1965
Catalog number: Grand Prix KS-426 (USA LP) mono (deleted)
Pickwick tracks: Ronnie Dickerson: Maybe Tomorrow (Philips-Vance-Sims-Reed), Love Can Make You Cry (Philips-Vance-Sims-Reed)
Musicians: not known
Producer: not known
Recording dates: 1965 (?)
Cover credit: not known
Of note: Grand Prix was another Pickwick label.

Various Artists/Out Of Sight!
Release date: 1967
Catalog number: Design 269 (USA LP) mono (deleted)
Pickwick tracks: Wonderful World Of Love (all written by Reed-Philips-Vance-Sims), Cycle Annie, Don't Turn My World Upside Down, Soul City
Musicians: Lou Reed (gtr, vcl on 2, perhaps others), plus studio musicians
Producer: not known
Recording dates: circa 1964
Cover credit: not known
Of note: 'Electronically enhanced' stereo – in other words, mono tracks with echo added.

All Night Workers: Don't Put Your Eggs In One Basket (Bill Alniger)/Why Don't You Smile Now? (Cale-Reed-Philips-Vance)
Release date: July 1965
Catalog number: Round Sound 1 (USA 45) mono (deleted)
Musicians: Lloyd Baskin, Peter Stampfel, Mike Esposito
Producer: not known
Recording dates: circa 1964
Cover credit: no cover
Of note: 1. Baskin, Stampfel and Esposito were Syracuse-area mates of Lou's. 2. Baskin went on to **Seatrain**, Stampfel to the **Fugs**, **Holy Modal Rounders**, and a solo career, and Esposito went to the **Blues Magoos**.

Donnie Burks: Why Don't You Smile Now? (Cale-Reed-Philips-Vance)/Satisfaction Guaranteed (not known)
Release date: 1965
Catalog number: Decca 32134 (USA 45) mono (deleted)
Musicians: Donnie Burks, plus others
Producer: Terry Philips
Recording dates: 1965
Cover credit: no cover
Of note: Burks was a Pickwick co-worker of Lou's.

PRE-VELVET UNDERGROUND SONGS WRITTEN BY LOU REED

Pre-Pickwick:

Sonata No.1 For Violin And Piano
Writer: Reed
Publisher: Lewis Reed
Date Registered: 7 October 1957
Of note: All the different spellings of Lou/Lewis/Louis are as they appear on the copyright forms filled out by Lou himself. (Mr. Reed's 'real' first names are Lewis Allen.)

Leave Her For Me
Writer: Reed
Publisher: Kempto Music
Date Registered: 28 November 1958

So Blue
Writers: Phil Harris (words), Lewis Reed (music)
Publisher: Kempto Music
Date Registered: 28 November 1958

You'll Never, Never Love Me
Writers: Louis Reed (words), Larry Allen (music)
Publisher: Louis A. Reed
Date Registered: 24 August 1959

Your Love
Writer: Reed
Publisher: Louis Reed
Date Registered: 6 March 1962

Pickwick:

Oh No, Don't Do It
Writers: Terry Philips-Jerry Vance-Jimmie Sims & Lew Reed
Publisher: Barmour Music
Date Registered: 16 November 1964
Of note: While at Pickwick, Reed wrote many songs with the Philips-Vance-Sims team. Little is known of these Pickwick co-workers, except that Terry Philips is really Philip Teitelbaum, and worked later with Phil Spector. Jerry Vance is really Jerry Pellegrino, and Jimmie Sims is really James N. Smith.

The Ostrich
Writers: Philips-Vance-Sims-Reed
Publisher: Barmour Music
Date Registered: 16 November 1964

I've Got A Tiger In My Tank
Writers: Robert Motta-Philips-Vance-Sims-Reed
Publisher: Barmour Music
Date Registered: 16 November 1964

Sneaky Pete
Writers: Philips-Vance-Sims-Reed
Publisher: Barmour Music
Date Registered: 16 November 1964

What About Me?
Writers: Philips-Vance-Sims-Reed
Publisher: Barmour Music
Date Registered: 16 November 1964

The Wild Ones
Writers: Philips-Vance-Sims-Reed
Publisher: Barmour Music
Date Registered: 16 November 1964

Help Me
Writers: Philips-Vance-Sims-Reed
Publisher: Barmour Music
Date Registered: 30 December 1964

Baby, You're The One
Writers: Philips-Vance-Sims-Reed
Publisher: Barmour Music
Date Registered: 13 January 1965

Bad Guy
Writers: Philips-Vance-Sims-Reed
Publisher: Barmour Music
Date Registered: 13 January 1965

Say Goodbye Over The Phone
Writers: Philips-Vance-Sims-Reed
Publisher: Barmour Music
Date Registered: 13 January 1965

Don't Turn My World Upside Down
Writers: Philips-Vance-Sims-Reed
Publisher: Barmour Music
Date Registered: 15 September 1965

Flowers For The Lady
Writers: Maurice Irby-Philips-Vance-Sims-Reed
Publisher: Barmour Music
Date Registered: 15 September 1965

Johnny Won't Surf No More
Writers: Philips-Vance-Sims-Reed
Publisher: Barmour Music
Date Registered: 15 September 1965

I'm Gonna Fight
Writers: Philips-Vance-Sims-Reed
Publisher: Barmour Music
Date Registered: 15 September 1965

Love Can Make You Cry
Writers: Philips-Vance-Sims-Reed
Publisher: Barmour Music
Date Registered: 15 September 1965

Maybe Tomorrow
Writers: Philips-Vance-Sims-Reed
Publisher: Barmour Music
Date Registered: 15 September 1965
Of note: This was recorded by 'Robertha Williams' and issued as a single, b/w **Tell Mama Not To Cry**, in 1965.

Soul City
Writers: Philips-Vance-Sims-Reed
Publisher: Barmour Music
Date Registered: 15 September 1965

Teardrops In The Sand
Writers: Philips-Vance-Sims-Reed
Publisher: Barmour Music
Date Registered: 15 September 1965

Tell Mama Not To Cry
Writers: Philips-Vance-Sims-Reed
Publisher: Barmour Music
Date Registered: 15 September 1965

This Rose
Writers: Philips-Vance-Sims-Reed
Publisher: Barmour Music
Date Registered: 15 September 1965

Ya Runnin' But I'll Get Ya
Writers: Philips-Vance-Sims-Reed
Publisher: Barmour Music
Date Registered: 15 September 1965

You're Driving Me Insane
Writers: Philips-Vance-Sims-Reed
Publisher: Barmour Music
Date Registered: 15 September 1965

Why Don't You Smile Now
Writers: Cale-Reed-Philips-Vance
Publisher: Barmour Music
Date Registered: 15 September 1965
Of note: This was recorded by the All Night Workers, the band of Lou's college friend Mike Esposito, and later by the English band The Downliners Sect on their last album for Columbia – the first time a Reed composition appeared in the UK.

Velvet Underground Discographies

45s AND EPs (ALL DELETED)

Note: All US unless noted.
The record companies, for the most part, picked the 45s. Thus these are an odd mix of the bizarre and the could-have-been-hits-ifs... The hardest thing to find out about the 45s has been which ones were actually released to the public. Often labels will release a 45 as a promo first; if it doesn't generate interest/airplay, end of story. The three Verve 45s definitely did come out as regular stock copies however.

All Tomorrow's Parties (Reed) (2:45)/**I'll Be Your Mirror** (Reed) (2:08)
Release date: 1966
Catalog number: Verve 10427 (USA 45) mono
Musicians: John Cale (electric viola, piano, bass), Sterling Morrison (rhythm gtr, bass), Nico (chanteuse), Lou Reed (lead gtr, ostrich gtr, vcl), Maureen Tucker (dms)
Producer: Andy Warhol
Recording dates: May 1966
Cover credit: Andy Warhol
Of note: 1. Some rare copies came in a picture sleeve with a photograph of the band by Andy.
2. **Parties** is edited to 2:45, and has a hotter, sonically-boosted mix than the LP version.
3. This 45 peaked at #103 on the Cashbox singles chart.

Sunday Morning (Reed) (2:53)/**Femme Fatale** (Reed) (2:35)
Release date: 1966
Catalog number: Verve 10466 (USA 45) mono
Musicians: John Cale (electric viola, piano, bass), Sterling Morrison (rhythm gtr, bass), Nico (chanteuse), Lou Reed (lead gtr, ostrich gtr, vcl), Maureen Tucker (dms)
Producer: 1 – Tom Wilson. 2 – Andy Warhol.
Recording dates: May 1966
Cover credit: no cover
Of note: This and the **Mirror** 45 were released before the first LP.

Loop (Cale) (6:49, or infinity)
Release date: December 1966
Catalog number: none (USA 7" flexi-disc) mono
Musicians: John Cale (bass, amplifier), Lou Reed (gtr?)
Producer: not known
Recording dates: 1964(?)
Cover credit: no cover
Of note: This came free in the December 1966 issue of **Aspen Magazine**. Warhol guest-edited the issue, and Lou contributed an essay on his view of rock & roll from the bandstand: "Life among the Poobahs, or 'I love you Eddie/but so does Betty/'cause you're such a handsome guy...'" **Loop** was the b-side. Side one was **White Wind**, a 'love raga' by Peter Walker, "Musical Director for Timothy Leary's LSD 'Religious Celebrations.'" **Loop** ends with a closed groove, hence the infinity timing.

Untitled (4:28)
Release date: February 1967
Catalog number: none (USA 7" flexi-disc) mono
Musicians: Nico (voice) Lou Reed (voice), among others at a party.
Producer: not known
Recording dates: 1967
Cover credit: no cover
Of note: This spontaneously-recorded conversation on a one-sided cardboard picture record showing a photograph of Reed was part of Warhol's **Index**.

Femme Fatale (Reed) (2:35)/**All Tomorrow's Parties** (Reed) (2:45)
Release date: 1967
Catalog number: Verve V-5138 (Australia 45) mono
Musicians: John Cale (electric viola, piano, bass), Sterling Morrison (rhythm gtr, bass), Nico (chanteuse), Lou Reed (lead gtr, ostrich gtr, vcl), Maureen Tucker (dms)
Producer: Andy Warhol
Recording dates: May 1966
Cover credit: no cover
Of note: 1. **Parties** is cut to 2:45, and has a hotter, sonically-boosted mix than the album version.
2. Orange Verve label.

Sunday Morning (Reed) (2:35)/ **I'll Be Your Mirror** (Reed) (2:08)
Release date: 1967
Catalog number: Verve V-? (Australia 45) mono
Musicians: John Cale (electric viola, piano, bass), Sterling Morrison (rhythm gtr, bass), Nico (chanteuse), Lou Reed (lead gtr, ostrich gtr, vcl), Maureen Tucker (dms)
Producer: Andy Warhol
Recording dates: May 1966
Cover credit: no cover
Of note: Orange Verve label.

All Tomorrow's Parties (Reed) (2:45)/**I'll Be Your Mirror** (Reed) (2:08)
Release date: 1967
Catalog number: Verve V-? (Canada 45) mono
Musicians: John Cale (electric viola, piano, bass), Sterling Morrison (rhythm gtr, bass), Nico (chanteuse), Lou Reed (lead gtr, ostrich gtr, vcl), Maureen Tucker (dms)
Producer: Andy Warhol
Recording dates: May 1966
Cover credit: no cover
Of note: **Parties** is cut to 2:45, and has a hotter, sonically-boosted mix than the album version.

White Light/White Heat (Reed) (2:44) / **Here She Comes Now** (Reed-Cale-Morrison-Tucker) (2:00)
Release date: February 1968
Catalog number: Verve 10560 (USA 45) mono
Musicians: John Cale (vcl, electric viola, organ, bass), Sterling Morrison (vcl, gtr, bass), Lou Reed (vcl, gtr, piano), Maureen Tucker (dms)
Producer: Tom Wilson
Recording dates: September 1967
Cover credit: no cover
Of note: It has long been said that there was a 45 of **Here She Comes Now/ I Heard Her Call My Name** but no evidence that this was released has been found.

What Goes On (Reed-D.Yule-Morrison-Tucker) (2:40) / **Jesus** (Reed-D.Yule-Morrison-Tucker) (3:24)
Release date: March 1969
Catalog number: MGM 14057 (USA 45) mono
Musicians: Sterling Morrison (vcl, gtr, bass), Lou Reed (vcl, gtr, piano), Maureen Tucker (dms), Doug Yule (vcl, kbds, bass)
Producer: Tom Wilson
Recording dates: September 1967
Cover credit: no cover
Of note: 1. This may have been a promo-only release.
2. WGO is shortened (faded) to 2:40.
3. **Jesus** is listed as being 2:55 on the label, but is in fact 3:24, same as on the LP.
4. These are the only mono mixes from the third LP.

Who Loves The Sun (Reed) (2:50) / **Oh! Sweet Nuthin'** (Reed) (7:23)
Release date: March 1971
Catalog number: Cotillion 44107 (USA 45) stereo
Musicians: Sterling Morrison (gtr), Lou Reed (gtr, piano, vcl), Billy Yule (dms), Doug Yule (organ, piano, bass, dms, lead gtr, gtr, vcl)
Producer: Geoffrey Haslam, Shel Kagan, The Velvet Underground
Recording dates: June 1970

Cover credit: no cover
Of note: The promo copy has **Sun** in mono, making it the last mono VU record (not counting **Max's**) and the only mono release from **Loaded**.

Who Loves the Sun (Reed) (2:50)/**Sweet Jane** (Reed) (3:15)
Release date: May 1971
Catalog number: Atlantic 2091-088 (UK 45) stereo
Musicians: Sterling Morrison (gtr), Lou Reed (gtr, piano, vcl), Billy Yule (dms), Doug Yule (organ, piano, bass, dms, lead gtr, gtr, vcl)
Producer: Geoffrey Haslam, Shel Kagan, The Velvet Underground
Recording date: June 1970
Cover credit: no cover
Of note: Atlantic name, Polydor catalog number, released under license from Atlantic, with red label.

Head Held High (Reed) (2:56)/**Train Round The Bend** (Reed) (3:20)
Release date: 1972
Catalog number: Cotillion 650.216 L (France 45) stereo
Musicians: Sterling Morrison (gtr), Lou Reed (gtr, piano, vcl), Billy Yule (dms), Doug Yule (organ, piano, bass, dms, lead gtr, gtr, vcl)
Producer: Geoffrey Haslam, Shel Kagan, The Velvet Underground
Recording date: June 1970
Cover credit: not known
Of note: Picture sleeve featuring the **Loaded** cover drawing, with 'Train Round The Bond' [sic] printed on top.

Sweet Jane (Reed) (3:15)/**Rock and Roll** (Reed) (4:39)
Release date: 1973
Catalog number: Atlantic K 10339 (UK 45) stereo
Musicians: Sterling Morrison (gtr), Lou Reed (gtr, piano, vcl), Billy Yule (dms), Doug Yule (organ, piano, bass, dms, lead gtr, gtr, vcl)

Producer: Geoffrey Haslam, Shel Kagan, The Velvet Underground
Recording date: June 1970
Cover credit: no cover
Of note: 1. Recalled due to technical problems with the pressing.
2. First record to use the 'VU featuring Lou Reed' billing.

I'm Waiting For The Man (Reed) (4:30)/**There She Goes Again** (Reed) (2:30)
Release date: 1973
Catalog number: MGM 2006 067 (Germany 45) stereo
Musicians: John Cale (electric viola, piano, bass), Sterling Morrison (rhythm gtr, bass), Lou Reed (lead gtr, ostrich gtr, vcl), Maureen Tucker (dms)
Producer: Andy Warhol
Recording dates: May 1966
Cover credit: not known
Of note: 'Lips and coke bottle' pop-art-style picture sleeve from the double LP compilation **Andy Warhol's Velvet Underground with Nico**.

Sweet Jane (Reed) (3:15)/**Rock and Roll** (Reed) (4:32)
Release date: March 1973
Catalog number: Atlantic 10 339 (Germany 45) stereo
Musicians: Sterling Morrison (gtr), Lou Reed (gtr, piano, vcl), Billy Yule (dms), Doug Yule (organ, piano, bass, dms, lead gtr, gtr, vcl)
Producer: Geoffrey Haslam, Shel Kagan, The Velvet Underground
Recording date: June 1970
Cover credit: not known
Of note: Purple picture sleeve with photograph of Reed playing live on his 1972 European tour.

I'm Waiting For The Man (Reed) (4:35)/**Run Run Run** (Reed) (4:16)/**Candy Says** (Reed-Morrison-Tucker-D.Yule) (4:09)
Release date: 1973

Catalog number: MGM 2006-283 (UK 7" EP) stereo
Musicians: 1,2 – John Cale (electric viola, piano, bass), Sterling Morrison (rhythm gtr, bass), Lou Reed (lead gtr, ostrich gtr, vcl), Maureen Tucker (dms). 3 – Sterling Morrison (vcl, gtr, bass), Lou Reed (vcl, gtr, piano), Maureen Tucker (dms), Doug Yule (vcl, kbds, bass).
Producer: 1,2 – Andy Warhol. 3 – The Velvet Underground.
Recording dates: 1,2 – May 1966; 3 – June 1970
Cover credit: no cover

I'm Waiting For The Man (Reed) (4:35) / **Candy Says** (Reed-Morrison-Tucker-D.Yule) (4:09) / **White Light/ White Heat** (Reed) (2:44)
Release date: 1973
Catalog number: MGM 2006 316 (Neth. 7" EP) stereo
Musicians: 1 – John Cale (electric viola, piano, bass), Sterling Morrison (rhythm gtr, bass), Lou Reed (lead gtr, ostrich gtr, vcl), Maureen Tucker (dms). 2 – John Cale (vcl, elect viola, organ, bass), Sterling Morrison (vcl, gtr, bass), Lou Reed (vcl, gtr, piano), Maureen Tucker (dms). 3 – Sterling Morrison (vcl, gtr, bass), Lou Reed (vcl, gtr, piano), Maureen Tucker (dms), Doug Yule (vcl, kbds, bass).
Producer: 1 – Andy Warhol. 2 – Tom Wilson. 3 – The Velvet Underground.
Recording dates: 1 – May 1966. 2 – June 1970. 3 – September 1966.
Cover credit: not known
Of note: Picture sleeve featuring photograph of Reed circa 1972.

I'm Waiting For The Man (Reed) (4:35) / **Run Run Run** (Reed) (4:16)
Release date: 1973
Catalog number: MGM 2006 310 (Germany 45) stereo
Musicians: John Cale (electric viola, piano, bass), Sterling Morrison (rhythm gtr, bass), Lou Reed (lead gtr, ostrich gtr, vcl), Maureen Tucker (dms)
Producer: Andy Warhol

Recording dates: May 1966
Cover credit: not known
Of note: 1. This 45 comes billed on the sleeve and record as 'Lou Reed and the Velvet Underground.'
2. The picture sleeve is a glam-rock style item, showing Lou in solo eye-makeup days.

I'm Waiting For The Man (Reed) (4:37) / **Venus In Furs** (Reed) (5:07)
Release date: 1978
Catalog number: Arista ARIST 12198 (UK 12" EP) stereo
Musicians: John Cale (electric viola, piano, bass), Sterling Morrison (rhythm gtr, bass), Lou Reed (lead gtr, ostrich gtr, vcl), Maureen Tucker (dms)
Producer: Andy Warhol
Recording dates: May 1966
Cover credit: not known
Of note: 1. This EP's A-side carries the full version of Reed's **Street Hassle**.
2. These are the original stereo mixes of these songs, making this 12" the best place to hear the songs other than on the mono LP. Great sound.

I'm Waiting For The Man (Reed) (4:37)
Release date: 1978
Catalog number: Arista ARIST 198 (UK 45) stereo
Musicians: John Cale (electric viola, piano, bass), Sterling Morrison (rhythm gtr, bass), Lou Reed (lead gtr, ostrich gtr, vcl), Maureen Tucker (dms)
Producer: Andy Warhol
Recording date: May 1966
Cover credit: no cover
Of note: This 45's A-side is Reed's **Street Hassle** edited to 4:02.

I'm Waiting For The Man (Reed) (4:37)/**Heroin** (Reed) (4:21)
Release date: 1980 (?)
Catalog number: Polydor 2095 399 (Germany 45) stereo
Musicians: John Cale (electric viola, piano, bass), Sterling Morrison (rhythm gtr, bass), Lou Reed (lead gtr, ostrich gtr, vcl), Maureen Tucker (dms)
Producer: Andy Warhol
Recording dates: May 1966
Cover credit: not known
Of note: 1. **Heroin** is cut to 4:21.
2. This was released in the Super Oldies series, with the original chart position reached shown on the back. These songs rate '...' – no chart entry.

Heroin (Reed) (7:07)/**Venus In Furs** (Reed) (5:07)/**I'm Waiting For The Man** (Reed) (4:35)
Release date: 1982
Catalog number: Polydor POSPX 603 (UK 12" EP) stereo
Musicians: John Cale (electric viola, piano, bass), Sterling Morrison (rhythm gtr, bass), Lou Reed (lead gtr, ostrich gtr, vcl), Maureen Tucker (dms)
Producer: Andy Warhol
Recording dates: May 1966
Cover credit: Pencil (– artist's pen name)
Of note: These are the original stereo mixes.

Foggy Notion (Reed) (3:50)/**I Can't Stand It** (Reed) (3:25)
Release date: February 1985
Catalog number: Polygram PRO 349-1 (USA promo 12") stereo
Musicians: Sterling Morrison (rhythm gtr, bass), Lou Reed (gtr, vcl), Maureen Tucker (dms), Doug Yule (vcl, kbds, bass)
Producer: The Velvet Underground
Recording dates: May 1969
Cover credit: not known
Of note: **Foggy** is faded to 3:50.

Stephanie Says (Reed) (2:49)
Release date: February 1985
Catalog number: Polydor SOUND 4 (UK 7" EP) stereo
Musicians: John Cale (electric viola, piano, bass), Sterling Morrison (gtr, bass), Lou Reed (gtr, vcl), Maureen Tucker (dms)
Producer: The Velvet Underground
Recording dates: February 1968
Cover credit: not known
Of note: This track is on a promo-only sampler EP given away free with the October 1986 issue of **Sounds** magazine.

I'm Waiting For The Man (Reed) (4:35)/**Heroin** (Reed) (7:05)
Release date: 1988
Catalog number: Old Gold OG 4049 (UK 12") stereo
Musicians: John Cale (electric viola, piano, bass), Sterling Morrison (rhythm gtr, bass), Lou Reed (lead gtr, ostrich gtr, vcl), Maureen Tucker (dms)
Producer: Andy Warhol
Recording dates: May 1966
Cover credit: Pencil

Venus In Furs (Reed) (5:06)/**All Tomorrow's Parties** (Reed) (5:55)
Release date: 1988
Catalog number: Old Gold OG 4051 (UK 12") stereo
Musicians: John Cale (electric viola, piano, bass), Sterling Morrison (rhythm gtr, bass), Nico (chanteuse, on 2), Lou Reed (lead gtr, ostrich gtr, vcl), Maureen Tucker (dms)
Producer: Andy Warhol
Recording dates: May 1966
Cover credit: Pencil
Of note: **Parties** is the single-voice Nico version.

Original LP Releases

The Velvet Underground & Nico
Release date: March 1967 (USA) October 1967 (UK)
Original catalog numbers:
   Verve V-5008 (mono), V6-5008 (stereo) (USA LP, 8-track)
   Verve M/VLP 9184 (mono) S/VLP (stereo) (UK LP)
   Polydor 2315 056 (UK) (1971 reissue with printed banana gatefold, US MGM LP)
Current reissue:
   PolyGram 823 290 (USA LP, cassette and CD)
Side 1/Sunday Morning (Reed) (2:51), I'm Waiting For The Man (Reed) (4:37), Femme Fatale (Reed) (2:35), Venus In Furs (Reed) (5:07), Run Run Run (Reed) (4:18), All Tomorrow's Parties (Reed) (5:55). *Side 2*/Heroin (Reed) (7:05), There She Goes Again (Reed) (2:36), I'll Be Your Mirror (Reed) (2:07), The Black Angel's Death Song (Reed/Cale) (3:10), European Son (Reed/Cale/Morrison/Tucker) (7:44)
Musicians: John Cale (electric viola, piano, bass), Sterling Morrison (rhythm gtr, bass), Nico (chanteuse), Lou Reed (lead gtr, ostrich gtr, vcl), Maureen Tucker (dms)
Producer: Andy Warhol, except **Sunday Morning** by Tom Wilson
Recording dates: May 1966
Cover credit: Andy Warhol
Of note: 1. The original US release came with a peel-off Warhol banana printed on the cover, and a small note to 'peel slowly and see.' When peeled, a pink banana was revealed.

2. Later reissues did away with the peelable covers, and simply printed a yellow banana instead.

3. Notable reissues:

– box (LP, CD) with booklet as part of HMV's Classics (UK, ltd. edition of 1500, C88 1-15, 1988).

– blue banana issue (Germany, Verve 2428 506, 1975; this was the inner pink banana cover shaded in blue).

– several Japanese issues have come with peelable bananas of varying quality.

– white vinyl (700 pressed), black vinyl (400) and a fine picture disc (1000) (Australia, Modern Records MOD-1001), 1990 – the first ever official VU color vinyl or picture disc.

– See Appendix for complete history.

White Light/White Heat
Release date: 30 January 1968 (USA) May 1968 (UK)
Original catalog numbers:
    Verve V-5046 (mono) V6-5046 (stereo) (USA LP, cassette, 8-track)
    Verve VLP 9201 (mono) SVLP 9201(stereo) (UK LP)
Current reissue:
    PolyGram 825 119 (LP, cassette, CD)
Side 1/White Light/White Heat (Reed) (2:44), The Gift (Reed/Morrison/Cale/Tucker) (8:14), Lady Godiva's Operation (Reed) (4:52), Here She Comes Now (Reed/Morrison/Cale/Tucker) (2:00). *Side 2*/I Heard Her Call My Name (Reed) (4:35), Sister Ray (Reed/Morrison, Cale, Tucker) (17:27)
Musicians: John Cale (vcl, electric viola, organ, bass), Sterling Morrison (vcl, gtr, bass), Lou Reed (vcl, gtr, piano), Maureen Tucker (dms)
Producer: Tom Wilson
Recording dates: September 1967
Cover credit: Billy Name (art), Andy Warhol (concept)
Of note: 1. 90% of the US albums with no skull on the cover are pirates, unlicensed copies made in the late 70s by a US record company that specialized, for a time, in turning out copies of a number of rare albums and then selling them as budget price cut-outs. Check the printing – if it looks fuzzy on the cover or the blue Verve label, it's

a pirate copy. However, a few *are* legit, as Verve reissued the record in the late 70s with a black label and left off the skull.

2. 1991 Australian issue (Modern Records MOD-1002) has the skull tattoo printed in black and the rest of the cover in grey so the skull is clearly visible. There are several varieties of this, as with their issue of the first LP: green vinyl, red multi-color splatter, yellow vinyl with a dash of red, and a picture disc showing the front and back covers, with original cover credits; small pressings of perhaps 1000 each.

3. UK history: Original UK issue came with skull, a 'flaps folded' back cover, and 'File Under: POPULAR: Pop Groups' printed on the back top margin. Also, the UK edition had the correct credits; earlier issues sometimes list the song **Here She Comes Now** as **There She Comes Now**, incorrectly credit Lou Reed with 'lead' guitar and fail to credit Andy Warhol for the cover – (the black-on-black was his idea). For the 1971 UK reissue a new cover was substituted, featuring a black and white photograph of toy soldiers, and this has been the UK cover ever since.

The Velvet Underground
Release date: March 1969 (USA) April 1969 (UK)
Original catalog numbers:
    MGM SE-4617 (USA muffled mix edition – LP, cassette, 8-track, reel-to-reel)
    MGM (UK) CS 8108 (Val Valentin mix LP)
    Polydor POL 340 2315 393 (France)
    all stereo
Current reissue:
    PolyGram 815 454 (LP, cassette, CD)
Side 1/Candy Says (all songs by The Velvet Underground: Reed/Morrison/Tucker/D.Yule) (4:01), What Goes On (4:30), Some Kinda Love (3:38), Pale Blue Eyes (5:41), Jesus (3:21). *Side 2*/Beginning To See The Light (4:29), I'm Set Free (4:01), That's The Story of My Life (2:00), The Murder Mystery (8:45), Afterhours (2:07)
Musicians: Sterling Morrison (gtr), Lou Reed (vcls, gtr), Maureen Tucker (dms), Doug Yule (vcl, bass, organ, piano)

Producer: The Velvet Underground
Recording date: November 1968
Cover credit: Billy Name
Of note: 1. There were two mixes of this LP, both in stereo. One was by Lou Reed, the so-called 'closet mix,' the other by MGM engineer Val Valentin (MGM's house engineer who usually worked on big band sessions for people such as Frank Sinatra), who did a fine, regular mix. Lou's mix also had a different take of **Some Kinda Love**. Lou's mix was the only one available in the US until the 1985 reissue. The Valentin mix was released in 1969 in the UK and Canada, then recalled, and replaced with a clearer version of Lou's mix.
2. The original French edition has **Beginning to See the Light** twice at the beginning of side two, an incredible oversight for a major record label.
3. UK history: issued with the Valentin mix in April 1969 (with back cover photograph cut in half horizontally rather than vertically). Reissued in 1971 with a sonically-boosted version of Lou's mix and the standard back cover.
4. The first German issue of the CD used in error one side of Lou's mix, side one from the album. Thus the different take of **Some Kinda Love** is included. The next pressing of the CD corrected this, and used the Valentin mix. The only way to tell the difference is the numbers around the CD's center hole: 01 is the first pressing, 02 is the second.

Loaded
Release date: September 1970 (USA) March 1971 (UK)
Original catalog numbers:
    Cotillion SD 9034 (USA LP, cassette, 8-track) stereo
    Atlantic K40113 (UK LP) stereo
Current reissue:
    Cotillion SD 9034 (USA LP, cassette)
    Warner Special Products 27613-2 (USA CD)
Side 1/Who Loves The Sun (all songs by Reed) (2:50), Sweet Jane (3:15), Rock & Roll (4:39), Cool It Down (3:05), New Age (4:39). *Side 2*/Head Held High (2:56), Lonesome Cowboy Bill (2:43), I Found A Reason (4:15), Train Round The Bend (3:20), Oh! Sweet Nuthin' (7:23)

Musicians: Sterling Morrison (gtr), Lou Reed (gtr, piano, vcl), Billy Yule (dms), Doug Yule (organ, piano, bass, dms, lead gtr, gtr, vcl)
Producer: Geoffrey Haslam, Shel Kagan, The Velvet Underground
Recording date: June 1970
Cover credit: Stanislaw Zagorski
Of note: 1. Moe is listed on the cover as playing percussion, but it's all Billy Yule.
2. On the Dutch issue (Atlantic ATL 40113) the smoke in the cover image is green instead of the usual red.

Live At Max's Kansas City
Release date: May 1972 (USA) August 1972 (UK)
Original catalog numbers:
>Cotillion SD 9500 (USA LP, cassette, 8-track) mono
>Atlantic K 30022 (UK LP) mono

Current reissue:
>Cotillion SD 9500 (LP, cassette)
>Atlantic 9500-2 (USA CD)
>Atlantic K30022 (UK LP)
>Atlantic 7567-90370-2 (Europe CD)

Side 1/I'm Waiting For The Man (all songs by Reed) (4:00), Sweet Jane (4:52), Lonesome Cowboy Bill (3:19), Beginning To See The Light (5:00). *Side 2*/I'll Be Your Mirror (1:55), Pale Blue Eyes (5:38), Sunday Morning (2:43), New Age (5:58), Femme Fatale (2:29), Afterhours (2:05)
Musicians: Sterling Morrison (gtr), Lou Reed (vcl, gtr), Billy Yule (dms), Doug Yule (bass, vcl)
Producer: Geoff Haslam
Recording date: 23 August 1970
Cover credit: Richard Mantel

Squeeze
Release date: February 1973
Original catalog number:
>Polydor 2383 180 (UK, Germany, Spain LP) stereo (deleted)

Side 1/Little Jack (all songs by Doug Yule) (3:35), Crash

(1:20), Caroline (2:32), Mean Old Man (2:53), Dopey Joe (3:06), Wordless (3:00). *Side 2*/She'll Make You Cry (2:45), Friends (2:38), Send No Letter (3:12), Jack & Jane (2:55), Louise (5:45)
Musicians: Ian Paice (dms), Doug Yule (vcl, gtr, bass, kbds)
Producer: Doug Yule
Recording dates: October, November 1972
Cover credit: not known

Live 1969
Release date: September 1974 (USA) February 1979 (UK)
Original catalog number:
    Mercury SRM 2-7504 (USA 2LPs, cass, 8-track) stereo
    Mercury 6641 900 (UK) stereo
Current reissue:
    PolyGram/Mercury SRM 2-7504 (USA 2LPs, cass)
    Mercury 834 823 (CD: Vol. 1)
    Mercury 834 824 (CD: Vol. 2)
    Mercury PRID 7 (UK 2LPs)
Side 1/I'm Waiting For The Man (all songs by Reed) (7:03), Lisa Says (5:52), What Goes On (8:55), Sweet Jane (4:00). *Side 2*/We're Gonna Have A Real Good Time Together (3:15), Femme Fatale (3:04), New Age (6:36), Rock & Roll (6:06), Beginning To See The Light (5:30), Heroin (8:14) (on Vol. 1 CD only). *Side 3*/Ocean (10:55), Pale Blue Eyes (5:51), Heroin (9:49). *Side 4*/Over You (2:17), Sweet Bonnie Brown/It's Just Too Much (7:55), White Light/White Heat (8:35), I Can't Stand It (7:51) (on Vol. 2 CD only), I'll Be Your Mirror (2:21)
Musicians: Sterling Morrison (gtr, vcl), Lou Reed (vcl, gtr), Maureen Tucker (dms), Doug Yule (bass, kbds)
Producer: Paul Nelson
Recording dates: October, November 1969
Cover credit: Ernst Thormahlen

VU
Release date: February 1985
Catalog numbers:
    PolyGram 823 299 (USA and Europe)

PolyGram 23 MM 0432 (Japan)
PolyGram 8237211 (Brazil)
PolyGram 823-721-2 (CD) (USA and Europe) stereo
Side 1/I Can't Stand It (all songs by Reed) (3:21), Stephanie Says (2:49), She's My Best Friend (2:46), Lisa Says (2:53), Ocean (5:09). *Side 2*/Foggy Notion (6:41), Inside Your Heart (2:29), One Of These Days (3:50), Andy's Chest (2:49), I'm Sticking With You (2:25)
Musicians: Sterling Morrison (gtr, vcl), Lou Reed (vcl, gtr), Maureen Tucker (dms), Doug Yule (kbds, bass, vcl). John Cale (viola, bass, kbds, vcl) replaces Yule on 2,7.
Recording dates: 2,7 – February 1968. 1,3,6,9,10 – May 1969. 5 – June 1969. 8 – September 1969. 4 – October 1969.
Cover credit: Larry Kazal
Of note: Pre-release cassettes sent to radio stations contained what was to be the original version of the album, with different mixes and with **Ferryboat Bill** in place of **Ocean**. (This version of **Ferryboat Bill** is different from the one eventually released on **Another View**.) The LP was then changed to the current version.

Another View
Release date: September 1986
Catalog number:
Verve/PolyGram 829 405 (USA and Europe LP, cassette, CD)
PolyGram POLD 5208 (UK LP)
Side 1/We're Gonna Have A Real Good Time Together (Reed) (2:56), I'm Gonna Move Right In (all other songs by The Velvet Underground) (6:30), Hey Mr. Rain (Version I) (4:39), Ride Into The Sun (3:25), Coney Island Steeplechase (2:20). *Side 2*/Guess I'm Falling In Love (3:28), Hey Mr. Rain (Version II) (5:25), Ferryboat Bill (2:10), Rock & Roll (5:14)
Musicians: Sterling Morrison (gtr), Lou Reed (vcls, gtr), Maureen Tucker (dms), Doug Yule (bass, vcls, kbds). John Cale (viola, bass, kbds) replaces Yule on 3,6,7
Producer: The Velvet Underground
Recording dates: 1,2,4 – September 1969. 3,7 – May 1968. 5 – May 1969. 6 – December 1967. 8,9 – June 1969.
Cover credit: George Corsillo

Unreleased Titles Copywritten by Lou Reed Whilst a Member of the Velvet Underground

Get It On Time
Writer: Reed
Publisher: Velvet Music
Date Registered: 22 April, 1966

Sweet-and-Twenty
Writers: William Shakespeare (words), Lou Reed (music)
Publisher: Lewis Reed
Date Registered: 10 June 1969

VU Compilations

Velvet Underground
Release date: 1970
Catalog number: MGM GAS 131 (USA LP) (deleted)
Side 1/Candy Says, Sunday Morning, Femme Fatale, White Light/White Heat, Jesus. *Side 2*/Heroin, Beginning To See The Light, Here She Comes Now, Afterhours
Cover credit: N. Jobst
Of note: Part of the 'Golden Archive' series.

Pop History (Frank Zappa and the Mothers of Invention/ The Velvet Underground featuring Nico)
Release date: 1970
Catalog number: Polydor 2335 033/4 (Germany 2 LPs) (deleted)
Side 1/White Light/White Heat, What Goes On, Venus In Furs, That's The Story of My Life, Here She Comes Now, Beginning To See The Light, Jesus. *Side 2*/Run Run Run, Some Kinda Love, The Gift, I'm Set Free, I Heard Her Call My Name. *Side 3* and *4* are The Mothers
Cover credit: not known

Superstarshine Vol. 20
Release date: 1970
Catalog number: Polydor METRO 2356 097 (Netherlands LP) (deleted)
Side 1/I'm Waiting For The Man, Sunday Morning, The Black Angel's Death Song, Here She Comes Now, There

She Goes Again, White Light/White Heat, Lady Godiva's Operation. *Side 2*/The Fairest of The Seasons (Nico), Winter Song (Nico), Eulogy To Lenny Bruce (Nico), Beginning To See The Light, Candy Says, Afterhours
Cover credit: not known
Of note: The Nico songs are from her **Chelsea Girl** LP.

Pop History Vol. 19
Release date: 1970
Catalog number: Polydor 2626 019 (Germany 2 LPs) (deleted)
Side 1/Lady Godiva's Operation, Eulogy To Lenny Bruce (Nico), What Goes On, Winter Song (Nico), Some Kinda Love. *Side 2*/The Gift, Chelsea Girl (Nico), I'm Set Free. *Side 3*/The Murder Mystery, Little Sister (Nico), I'll Be Your Mirror, Wrap Your Troubles In Dreams (Nico). *Side 4*/Jesus, The Fairest of The Seasons (Nico), After Hours, It Was A Pleasure Then (Nico), That's The Story of My Life
Cover credit: not known

Andy Warhol's Velvet Underground Featuring Nico
Release date: 1971
Catalog numbers:
MGM/Polydor METRO 2683 006 (German, UK 2 LPs, cassette, 8-track) (deleted)
Metro/DGG 2629 001 (France 2 LPs) (deleted)
Side 1/I'm Waiting For The Man, Candy Says, Run Run Run, White Light/White Heat, All Tomorrow's Parties. *Side 2*/Sunday Morning, I Heard Her Call My Name, Femme Fatale, Heroin, Here She Comes Now, There She Goes Again. *Side 3*/Sister Ray, Venus In Furs. *Side 4*/European Son, Pale Blue Eyes, The Black Angel's Death Song, Beginning To See The Light
Cover credit: Keith Davis/Grahame Berney
Of note: **1.** Cover carries a Warhol-style painting of a Coke bottle with straw and big lips.
2. Original UK and German covers were printed on very good quality paper.

Lou Reed and the Velvet Underground
Release date: October 1973
Catalog number: Pride/MGM PRD-0022 (USA LP) (deleted)
Side 1/That's The Story of My Life, Sister Ray, Lady Godiva's Operation. *Side 2*/Heroin, Sunday Morning, All Tomorrow's Parties, There She Goes Again, White Light/White Heat, Femme Fatale
Cover credit: not known
Of note: Excellent mastering and pressing, especially of **Sister Ray** and **Lady Godiva's Operation**.

Archetypes
Release date: 1974
Catalog number: MGM M3F-4950 (USA LP, cassette, 8-track) (deleted)
Side 1/White Light/White Heat, The Gift, Lady Godiva's Operation, Here She Comes Now. *Side 2*/I Heard Her Call My Name, Sister Ray
Cover credit: Ave Pildas, Miles Tilton, Nancy Young
Of note: Reissue of **White Light/White Heat**, with different, incongruous cover of two people standing in front of a Woolworth's store wearing motorcycle helmets.

Lou Reed and The Velvet Underground
Release date: 1974
Catalog number: MGM 2315 258 SUPER (UK, Germany LP, cassette, 8-track) (deleted)
Side 1/I'm Waiting For The Man, Sister Ray, Lady Godiva's Operation. *Side 2*/Heroin, Sunday Morning, All Tomorrow's Parties, There She Goes Again, White Light/White Heat, Femme Fatale
Cover credit: Hartmut Pfeiffer

Startrack No. 9
Release date: 1974
Catalog number: Metro/MGM/Polydor 2364 067 (Holland LP) (deleted)
Side 1/Heroin, What Goes On, Venus In Furs, That's The Story of My Life, Run Run Run. *Side 2*/Candy Says, Some Kinda Love, European Son, Jesus, I'm Set Free
Cover credit: Hartmut Pfeiffer

The Velvet Underground
Release date: 1975
Catalog number: MGM 2354 033 (UK LP, cassette) (deleted)
Side 1/White Light/White Heat, What Goes On, Venus In Furs, That's The Story of My Life, Here She Comes Now, Beginning To See The Light, Jesus. *Side 2*/Run Run Run, Some Kinda Love, The Gift, I'm Set Free, I Heard Her Call My Name
Cover credit: Keith Davis

Die Velvet Underground Story
Release date: 1975
Catalog number: Verve 2304 149 (Germany LP) (deleted)
Side 1/I'm Waiting For The Man, Run Run Run, Heroin, There She Goes Again, European Son, White Light/White Heat. *Side 2*/I Heard Her Call My Name, Candy Says, What Goes On, Some Kinda Love, Jesus, Pale Blue Eyes
Cover credit: not known
Of note: Gatefold LP in the 'Franz Scholer prasentiert series, with VU bio inside and Franz' on the back cover.

Pop History #12
Release date: 1975 (?)
Catalog number: Polydor 2612 021 (UK LP) (deleted)
Side 1/not known. *Side 2*/not known
Cover credit: not known

Pop Giants Vol. 9
Release date: 1976 (?)
Catalog number: Brunswick 2911 520 (Germany LP) (deleted)
Side 1/The Murder Mystery, I'm Set Free, Lady Godiva's Operation, Winter Song (Nico). *Side 2*/Wrap Your Troubles In Dreams (Nico), The Gift, Some Kinda Love, Eulogy To Lenny Bruce (Nico)
Cover credit: not known

The Story of... Velvet Underground
Release date: 1978
Catalog number: Polydor 2664 405 (Germany 2 LPs, cassette) (deleted)
Side 1/I'm Waiting For The Man, Candy Says, Run Run Run, White Light/White Heat, All Tomorrow's Parties. *Side 2*/Sunday Morning, I Heard Her Call My Name, Femme Fatale, Heroin, Here She Comes Now, There She Goes Again. *Side 3*/Sister Ray, Venus In Furs. *Side 4*/European Son, Pale Blue Eyes, The Black Angel's Death Song, Beginning To See The Light
Cover credit: not known

The Velvet Underground Featuring Lou Reed
Release date: 1978
Catalog number: Polydor 2664 438 (Germany 2 LP, cassette) (deleted)
Side 1/Lady Godiva's Operation, Eulogy To Lenny Bruce (Nico), What Goes On, Winter Song (Nico), Some Kinda Love. *Side 2*/The Gift, Chelsea Girl (Nico), I'm Set Free. *Side 3*/The Murder Mystery, Little Sister (Nico), I'll Be Your Mirror, Wrap Your Troubles In Dreams (Nico). *Side 4*/Jesus, The Fairest of The Seasons (Nico), After Hours, It Was A Pleasure Then (Nico), That's The Story of My Life
Cover credit: not known

The Velvet Underground and Lou Reed
Release date: 1980 (?)
Catalog number: Superstar SU 1012 (Italy LP) (deleted)
Side 1/Sister Ray, Venus In Furs. *Side 2*/European Son, Pale Blue Eyes, The Black Angel's Death Song, Beginning To See The Light
Cover credit: Vittorio Antinori

Historia De La Musica Rock #38:
    The Velvet Underground
Release date: 1982
Catalog number: Polydor 2861 301 (Spain)
Side 1/Sister Ray, Venus In Furs. *Side 2*/European Son, Pale Blue Eyes, The Black Angel's Death Song, Beginning To See The Light
Cover credit: not known
Of note: Black market issue with lyrics and history.

Masters of Rock...
    The Best Of The Velvet Underground
Release date: 1986
Catalog number: Team T 5838 (Indonesia cassette)
Side 1/I'm Waiting For The Man, I'll Be Your Mirror, Sunday Morning, White Light/White Heat, Candy Says, Run Run Run, Heroin, There She Goes Again. *Side 2*/ We're Gonna Have A Good Time Together, All Tomorrow's Parties, Lady Godiva's Operation, Femme Fatale, Venus In Furs, What Goes On, Rock & Roll
Cover credit: Stupa Pratamaraya

The Velvet Underground
Release date: July 1986
Catalog number: Polydor VUBOX 1/829-404-1 (UK/ Netherlands 5 LPs)
Record 1/**The Velvet Underground & Nico**
Record 2/**White Light/White Heat**
Record 3/**The Velvet Underground**

Record 4/**VU**
Record 5/**Another View**
Cover credit: not known
Of note: This was issued a few months prior to the release of **Another View**, and the version of that album in this set comes with a blank black cover and the titles and credits printed on the label.

The Best Of The Velvet Underground
(Words And Music Of Lou Reed)
Release date: 1989
Catalog number: Verve/PolyGram 841 164 (USA CD, cassette) (European LP, CD, cassette)
Side 1/I'm Waiting For The Man, Femme Fatale, Run Run Run, Heroin, All Tomorrow's Parties, I'll Be Your Mirror, White Light/White Heat, Stephanie Says. *Side 2*/What Goes On, Beginning To See The Light, Pale Blue Eyes, I Can't Stand It, Lisa Says, Sweet Jane, Rock & Roll
Cover credit: Audrey Bernstein
Of note: 1. An important release which stands as the best VU collection to date. It has the best VU sound ever (except for the elevated vocal levels on the tracks from the first LP) as it was mastered from original tapes, something which hasn't happened since the original LPs first came out. It also included some of the Atlantic material, for the first time in any legit collection.
2. Double-tracked vocal version of **All Tomorrow's Parties**.
3. 20 seconds longer fade-out on **What Goes On**, 10 seconds longer fade-outs on **I'm Waiting For The Man** and **Beginning To See The Light**.
4. Liner design by Gerard Malanga, with several rare photographs.

The Best Of The Velvet Underground
(Words And Music Of Lou Reed)
Release date: 1989
Catalog number: Green Club Riviera G.C. 1310 (Indonesia cassette)
Side 1/I'm Waiting For The Man, Femme Fatale, Run

Run Run, Heroin, All Tomorrow's Parties, I'll Be Your Mirror, White Light/White Heat, Stephanie Says. *Side 2*/What Goes On, Beginning To See The Light, Pale Blue Eyes, I Can't Stand It, Lisa Says, Sweet Jane, Rock & Roll
Cover credit: not known
Of note: Budget version of the above with generic tape and cheap one-sided slip cover.

The Velvet Underground
Release date: 1989
Catalog number: Verve/PolyGram 424 610 (Spain LP)
Side 1/Sunday Morning, I'm Waiting For The Man, Femme Fatale, Venus In Furs, Pale Blue Eyes. *Side 2*/ Heroin, All Tomorrow's Parties, White Light/White Heat, I'll Be Your Mirror
Cover credit: not known
Of note: LPs in this series, 'Rock – La Musics, Los Interpretes', include a 20 page glossy insert – but the VU/Lou Reed one comes inside Adam Ant's **Friend or Foe** LP (CBS LSP 982344 1). That's by design; with the VU record comes a book about the Moody Blues and progressive rock.

Velvet Underground
Release date: 1990
Catalog number: Verve/PolyGram 1135/136 (Italy CD)
Sunday Morning, I'm Waiting For The Man, Femme Fatale, Venus In Furs, I'll Be Your Mirror, Sweet Jane, Heroin, All Tomorrow's Parties, White Light/White Heat, Pale Blue Eyes
Cover credit: not known
Of note: #67 in the "Il Rock De Agostini" series.

The Velvet Underground
Release date: June 1990
Catalog number: Polydor 843 885.2 – Pol 929 (French 4 [or 5] CD box set)
CD 1/**The Velvet Underground & Nico**
CD 2/**White Light/White Heat**

CD 3/**The Velvet Underground**
CD 4/**VU**
CD 5/**The Velvet Underground:** 'Jingle Radio' (:58) (1969 radio ad for third LP), One Of These Days (3:22), Pale Blue Eyes (6:30), I'm Sticking With You (2:29) – live, Dallas, Texas, 28 October 1969, Ride Into The Sun (3:44) – 1969 demo, from acetate, with vocals
Musicians: Lou Reed (gtr, vcl), Sterling Morrison (gtr), Maureen Tucker (dms, vcl on CD 3), Doug Yule (bass, kbds, vcl). On CD 1 add Bill 'Rosko' Mercer, announcer).
Cover credit: Fred McDarrah
Of note: 1. Box set limited edition of 5000 commemorating the June 1990 Cartier Exhibition, including a glossy 32-page booklet, with large, rare, vintage photographs of the band, Andy Warhol and Edie Sedgwick.
2. The fifth CD (limited numbered edition of 3000) came with a peelable banana on the cover, and was distributed as a bonus in some record stores when you bought the box set.

The Velvet Underground (Superstars/Best Collection)
Release date: 1990
Catalog number: CR F-023 (Japan CD)
Run Run Run, I'm Waiting For The Man, Lisa Says, Sweet Jane, Femme Fatale, I'll Be Your Mirror, White Light/White Heat, What Goes On, Beginning To See The Light, I Can't Stand It, All Tomorrow's Parties, Rock & Roll
Cover credit: not known
Of note: 1. Same as the 1989 USA 'Best of' minus **Heroin**, **Stephanie Says** and **Pale Blue Eyes**.
2. The cover shows an early 70s blue-light photograph of Lou live.

Chronicles (Superstars/Best Collection)
Release date: 1990
Catalog number: CR F-023 (Australia CD)
Pale Blue Eyes, Beginning To See The Light, What Goes On, White Light/White Heat, Sunday Morning, I'm Waiting For The Man, Femme Fatale, Venus In Furs, Run Run Run, All Tomorrow's Parties, Heroin, I Can't Stand It, Stephanie Says, She's My Best Friend, Andy's Chest, Sweet Jane, Rock and Roll
Cover credit: not known
Of note: 1. Rock and Roll and **Sweet Jane** are from **Live 1969.**
2. Part of a mid-price Startrax series.

Velvet Underground Tracks on Compilations, Radio Shows, Spin-Offs Etc.

The East Village Other/Electric Newspaper/Hiroshima Day
Release date: August 1966
Catalog number: ESP 1034 (USA LP only) stereo (deleted)
VU Track: Noise (The Velvet Underground) (1:47)
Musicians: John Cale (bass), Maureen Tucker (dms), Sterling Morrison (gtr), Lou Reed (gtr)
Producer: not known
Recorded: 1966
Cover credit: Walter Bowart
Of note: 1. This VU track is improvised.
2. Other artists contributing to this 'protest' LP were Andy Warhol (Silence), Allen Ginsberg, Gerard Malanga, Ingrid Superstar, and the Fugs.
3. As with all ESP discs, there are label differences: the first issue has red and blue labels, the reissue black labels (with a misprint which credits the VU with **Gossip**) and a 'Stereo' sticker on the cover.
4. Reissued in bootleg, blank cover form in 1980.

The Music Factory
Release date: 1968
Original catalog number: MGM MFRS-3 (USA 2 LPs, promo-only) stereo (deleted)
VU Track: I'll Be Your Mirror

Participants: John Cale, Lou Reed, Tom Wilson
Producer: Tom Wilson
Recorded: 1968
Cover credit: not known
Of note: 1. 2 LPs of interviews and music from the latest, hippest Verve/MGM artists. Host: Tom Wilson.
2. The Reed-Cale sections were bootlegged in 1987 on **An Interview With The Velvet Underground** (Velvet 1), released as a picture disc; but side one was repeated on side two, and so only half the interview was presented.
3. Also includes an ad for Nico's **Chelsea Girl** LP, as well as **The Fairest of the Seasons** from that LP.

June Sampler LP
Release date: 1968
Original catalog number: MGM/Verve MVP 2 (UK promo-only) stereo (deleted)
VU Track: Here She Comes Now
Cover credit: not known
Of note: Also included on the LP: Johnny Tillotson (**Poetry In Motion**), Hank Williams, and The Cowsills.

'Not For Sale'
Release date: 1968 (?)
Catalog number: Polydor SPECIAL 1A (UK LP, promo-only) (deleted)
VU Tracks: Run Run Run, Beginning To See The Light
Cover credit: not known

What Goes On (Reed-D.Yule-Morrison-Tucker) 2:40/ **Beginning To See the Light** (Reed-D.Yule-Morrison-Tucker) 3:24
Release date: 1969
Catalog number: MGM VU-1 (USA 45) mono
Musicians: Bill 'Rosko' Mercer (announcer), Sterling Morrison (vcl, gtr, bass), Lou Reed (vcl, gtr, piano), Maureen Tucker (dms), Doug Yule (vcl, kbds, bass)
Producer: The Velvet Underground
Recording dates: September 1967
Cover credit: Billy Name
Of note: 1. Promo-only radio ad, with music.

2. The text was probably written by manager Steve Sesnick.
3. The PS carries the same photograph as on the cover of the third LP, but with the **Bazaar** magazine cover unretouched.

Underground
Release date: 1969
Catalog number: Polydor 1184 190/91 (Spain 2 LPs) (deleted)
VU Tracks: I'm Waiting For The Man, Sunday Morning, I Heard Her Call My Name, Here She Comes Now, European Son
Cover credit: not known
Of note: This was the first VU material ever to be released in Spain.

Entwicklung Der Pop Music, Vol. 2
Release date: 1969
Catalog number: DGG 2536016 (German LP) (deleted)
VU Track: I'm Waiting For The Man
Cover credit: not known
Of note: This collection was never available in record shops but was sold only through schools.

Pop Giants
Release date: 1969 (?)
Catalog number: Polydor 2482 260 (UK LP) (deleted)
VU Track: Heroin
Cover credit: not known
Of note: The cover says 'Heroin performed by Lou Reed', but it's the VU's version, faded out halfway through.

Rock Dreams
Release date: 1970
Catalog number: Polydor 2488 313 (Germany LP) (deleted)
VU Track: I'm Waiting For The Man
Cover credit: not known

Of note: This LP came in a package with the **Rock Dreams** book, which featured paintings of the VU and of a solo Lou by Guy Peellaert.

Hot Rock
Release date: 1972
Catalog number: PolyGram HR 002 (New Zealand 2 LPs) (deleted)
VU Track: Run Run Run
Cover credit: not known
Of note: Red vinyl.

Pop Giants
Release date: 1972 (?)
Catalog number: Polydor 184 190/1 (Germany LP) (deleted)
VU Tracks: I'm Waiting For The Man, Sunday Morning, I Heard Her Call My Name, Here She Comes Now, European Son
Cover credit: not known
Of note: Released in conjunction with **Der Stern** magazine.

Das Bleiben Hits II
Release date: 1974
Catalog number: Atlantic WEA 3-68009 (Germany 3 LPs promo only) (deleted)
VU Track: Sweet Jane
Cover credit: not known

Rock Of The USA
Release date: 1975
Catalog number: MGM (?) (UK LP) (deleted)
VU Track: I'm Waiting For The Man
Cover credit: not known

All You Need Is Love
Release date: 1975
Catalog number: Theatre Projects Records/Phonogram 9199 995 (UK LP, cassette) (deleted)

VU Track: I'm Waiting For The Man
Cover credit: not known
Of note: This was a tie-in with a British TV series. Even though **Waiting** was never mentioned on the program, here it is, right between **Apache** by the Shadows and Neil Sedaka's remake of **Breaking Up Is Hard To Do**.

Lou Reed/**Rock And Roll Diary 1967-1980**
Release date: 1980
Original catalog number: Arista A2L-8603 (USA 2 LPs, cassette)
Current catalog number: AL11-8434
VU Tracks: I'm Waiting For The Man, White Light/White Heat, I Heard Her Call My Name, Pale Blue Eyes, Beginning To See The Light, Sweet Jane, Rock & Roll, Heroin, Femme Fatale
Cover credit: not known

The Continuous History of Rock and Roll
Release date: January 1982
Catalog numbers: Rolling Stone Magazine Productions RSMP 82-14 (USA radio show on LP)
VU Track: Rock & Roll
Cover credit: not known
Of note: This is a portion of an 'East Coast Rock' USA radio show broadcast, and includes a brief interview with Lou.

Nico/**The Blue Angel**
Release date: August 1985 (UK)
Catalog numbers:
        Aura AUL 731 (UK LP, cassette, CD)
        Tonpress SX-T 90 (Poland LP)
VU Tracks: Femme Fatale, All Tomorrow's Parties
Cover credit: not known
Of note: 1. Nico retrospective.
2. This represents the first time any VU material was legitimately available in Eastern Europe.
3. The record was manufactured in Russia by Melodya and the cover made in Poland, with liner notes in English and Polish.

Electric Sixties
Release date: 1985
Catalog number: JCI-3103 (USA LP, cassette, CD)
VU Track: All Tomorrow's Parties
Cover credit: not known
Of note: Part of the 'Baby Boomer Classics' series.

Psychedelic Psnack
Release date: 4 May 1987
Catalog number: Westwood One Radio Networks PP 87-19 (USA radio show on LP)
VU Track: Sweet Jane
Cover credit: not known
Of note: Includes a brief interview with Lou.

Rolling Stone 20th Anniversary Salute
Release date: 1987
Catalog number: none (USA radio show on 3 LPs)
VU Tracks: I'm Waiting For The Man, Pale Blue Eyes
Cover credit: not known
Of note: From the 'Top 100 LPs' show.

Back On The Road
Release date: 1988
Catalog number: Stylus SMD 854 (UK LP/Cass.) mono
VU Track: Venus in Furs
Recorded: 1967
Cover credit: not known

Lou Reed/A Rock & Roll Life (Some of his Greatest Songs and a Personal Chat)
Release date: 1989
Catalog number: Sire PRO-CD-3358 (USA promo-only 2 CDs)
VU Tracks: Heroin, White Light/White Heat, Pale Blue Eyes, Rock & Roll
Cover credit: Maura P. McLaughlin
Of note: 1. Includes a 26-minute conversation with Lou about his record **New York**.
2. Limited edition of 3000.

Lou Reed/Retro
Release date: 1989
Catalog number: PD 90309 (Germany)
VU Tracks: Heroin, I'm Waiting for the Man
Cover credit: Stylorouge
Of note: VU tracks are on the CD and cassette, but not on the LP.

Flashback! – 1969
Air date: 1 January 1990
Catalog number: Show #157 (USA show "Radio Today" on 2 CDs)
VU Track: Rock & Roll
Cover credit: not known

Original Soundtrack/The Doors
Release date: March 1991
Catalog number: Elektra 9 61047 stereo
VU Track: Heroin
Cover credit: not known

The Psychedelic Years 1966-1969 –
       American Album Classics
Release date: 1990
Catalog number: Knight Records/Castle Communications PSDCD 47003 (3 LP, CD) stereo
VU Track: Venus In Furs
Cover credit: not known

John Cale/Paris S'Eveille Suivi d'Autres Compositions
Release date: December 1991
Catalog number: Les Disques du Crepuscule TWI 952 (Arista CD only)
VU Track: Booker T (The Velvet Underground) (edited version)
Musicians: John Cale (bass), Maureen Tucker (drums), Sterling Morrison (gtr), Lou Reed (gtr)
Producer: not known
Recorded: August 1967, recorded live at the Gymnasium, New York City

Cover credit: not known
Of note: **Booker T** is the music to **The Gift**, and is shortened here to 3:00.

John Cale/ **Paris S'Evielle**
Release date: December 1991
Catalog number: Les Disques De Crepuscule/ Delabel/ Virgin DE 035080 PM 515 (France CD EP only)
VU Track: Booker T (The Velvet Underground) (long version)
Musicians: John Cale (bass), Maureen Tucker (drums), Sterling Morrison (gtr), Lou Reed (gtr)
Producer: not known
Recorded: August 1967, recorded live at the Gymnasium, New York City
Cover credit: not known
Of note: This 'long version' of **Booker T** is 6:36.

The Vox Box
Release date: February 1992
Catalog number: Vox GIVIT2 (UK cassette only)
VU Track: Sweet Jane
Cover art: King Ink
Of note: 1. Promo sampler given away with the March 1992 issue of 'Vox' magazine.
2. This is the **Sweet Jane** from **Loaded**.

Zounds – Das Muzikmagazin
Release date: February 1992
Catalog number: (Germany CD only)
VU Tracks: I'm Waiting for the Man, Pale Blue Eyes
Cover credit: King Ink
Of note: Promo sampler given away by the publishers of **Zounds**.

Records of Related Interest

68/ WRKO (Now Radio In Boston) Presents 30 Now Goldens
Release date: 1968 (?)
Catalog number: Post 68 (USA 2 LPs) (deleted)
Cover credit: not known
Of note: No VU music is to be found on this good Top 40 hits collection, but inside there is a fine photograph of one of the WRKO DJs standing at the mic in front of Lou, Sterling and John and their Vox amps. They look to be tuning up, he looks to be introducing them. A good glimpse of the atmosphere in which the VU were working in 1968.

The Velvet Underground: Somebody To Love (Darby Slick) (2:40)/**She Comes In Colors** (Arthur Lee) (3:10)
Release date: January 1970
Catalog number: Festival Records FK-3466 (Australia 45) mono (deleted)
Musicians: Steve Phillopson, Herm Kovacs, Steve Crothers, Tony Heads, Les Hall
Producer: not known
Recording dates: 1969 (?)
Cover credit: none
Of note: This 'Velvet Underground' was an Australian band who said they also got their name from the book by Michael Leigh.

So You Wanna Be A Rock 'N' Roll Star, Volume 2/ The Psychedelic Years of Australian Rock 1967-1970
Release date: mid-70s
Catalog number: Festival Records L45705/6 (Australia 2LPs) stereo (deleted)
'VU' Track: Somebody To Love (Darby Slick) (2:40)
Musicians: Steve Phillopson, Herm Kovacs, Steve Crothers, Tony Heads, Les Hall
Producer: not known
Recorded: 1969?
Cover credit: not known
Of note: 1. LP compiled by Glenn A. Baker.
2. With photograph and short bio of the Australian VU: "It has been suggested that Newcastle's Velvet Underground were responsible for selling more Doors records in Australia than the group themselves. As with the Australian Rotary Connection, Velvet Underground claim complete ignorance of any American usage of their title, having lifted it (like Reed, Cale and Co.) from the book of the same name – essential 'head' reading in 1967. As premier rock act in that rowdy industrial city between 1967-70, the Velvets were 'dedicated followers of fashion,' offering quality versions of material by Love, Jefferson Airplane, The Doors and others of similar ilk. Fronted by Steve Phillopson, a pioneer in the use of 'lighter fluid theatrics,' the group comprised Herm Kovacs, Russell Bayne (to Pyramid), Mark Priest and David Schofield. Upon departure of the latter three, Steve Crothers, Tony Heads (both of Taxi) and Les Hall joined to form the recording line up. Later members included Andy Imlah (from Elm Tree), Malcolm Young (AC/DC) and Brian Johnson. The final two years of the group's lifespan (1971-72) found them based in Sydney as a much-demanded suburban dance band. A situation which threw them together with pop soloist Ted Mulry, who often utilized them as a backing unit. Friendships developed to the point where Kovacs and Hall joined with Mulry in September 1972 at Newcastle's Waitara Festival, as The Ted Mulry Gang, which, with the subsequent addition of Fat Harry's Gary Dixon, has emerged as one of the mid 70's more popular teenage bands."

Polish VU Postcards
These come from a fellow in Poland (K3 Records) who has a machine at home that lets him take a postcard, play a record, and etch the song onto a plastic coating on the postcard. These bootleg oddities exist in limited quantity, usually in numbered sets of 50. I've seen VU cards of **I'm Waiting For The Man** and **I'm Gonna Move Right In**. There are also Nico postcards of **Femme Fatale**, **I'm Waiting For The Man**, **60/40**, and **I'll Keep It With Mine**. Some of the postcards carry VU/Warhol-related pictures, others are just tourist cards.

Velvet Underground-inspired Paintings
Arie Houtman, a Dutch artist, has done a wonderful series of abstract paintings titled after or inspired by VU and Lou Reed songs. There is a 'Sister Ray System Series', and many others such as 'The Gift', 'Venus In Furs', and 'The Black Angel's Death Song'.

COVER VERSIONS

Cover Versions of Velvet Underground Songs

Artist	VU Song Covered	Location (Record Label, Format, Date)
Absent Music	*Pale Blue Eyes*	Absent Music For Absent People (Cass., 1986)
Absolute Grey	*Beginning To See The Light*	Greenhouse (v.a.) (Earring, LP, 1985)
Acid Flowers	*The Black Angel's Death Song*	Andy Warhol (v.a.) (Sub-Up, LP/CD, 1987)
Afflicted, The	*Sweet Jane*	(LP, 1986)
Age of Chance	*All Tomorrow's Parties*	(LP)
Alberto Y Los Trios Paranoias	*Heroin*	Alberto Y Los Trios Paranoias (Transatlantic Records, LP, 197?)
Christi, Angel Corpus	*Femme Fatale*	I Love NY (LP, 1985)
Badgemen	*Sister Ray*	Heaven and Hell, vol III (v.a.) (Imaginary, LP/CD/Cass., 1992)
Beach Bullies	*Femme Fatale*	We Rule The Universe (Musclebound Records, LP, 1980)
Beat Farmers, The	*There She Goes Again*	Tales of the New West (Rhino, LP, 1985)

ARTIST	VU SONG COVERED	LOCATION (RECORD LABEL, FORMAT, DATE)
Beat Temptation	What Goes On	Concerned About Rock Music? (Homestead, LP, 1986)
Beatitudes, The	I'll Be Your Mirror	A History of Nothing (Buro, LP, 1985)
Beef	Femme Fatale	Heaven and Hell, vol II (v.a.) (Imaginary, LP/CD/Cass., 1991)
Bickers, Terry & Bradleigh Smith	I'm Set Free	Heaven and Hell, vol I (v.a.) (UK: Imaginary/ USA: Communion, LP/CD, 1991)
Big Balls & The Great White Idiot	White Light/White Heat	Big Balls & The Great White Idiot (Nova, LP, 1977)
Big Star	Femme Fatale	Sister Lovers (PVC, LP/CD, 1978)
Black Britain	Heroin	Heroin (45, 1988)
Black Carnations	What Goes On	Raw Cuts, Vol. 3 (v.a.) (LP/CD, 1987)
Blackbird	What Goes On	Blackbird (Ikoki, LP, 1989)
Blood & Roses	I'm Waiting for the Man	(Cass., 197?)
Blue Aeroplanes	Sweet Jane	World View Blue (EP, 1990)
Blue Suede	Rock & Roll	Out of the Blue (EMI, LP, 1975)
Bodan X	I'm Waiting for the Man	(Jungle, 45, 1984)
Bollock Brothers, The	The Gift	The Last Supper (Charly Records, 2LP, 1983)

ARTIST	VU SONG COVERED	LOCATION (RECORD LABEL, FORMAT, DATE)
Bombay Ducks	*There She Goes Again*	Dance Music (LP, 1981)
Bowie, David	*White Light/White Heat*	Ziggy Stardust/The Motion Picture (RCA, LP, 1983)
Brood, Herman & His Wild Romance	*I Can't Stand It*	Cha Cha (Ariola, LP, 1978)
Brownsville Station	*Sweet Jane*	Smokin' In The Boy's Room (Bell/Big Tree, LP, 1973)
Buffalo Tom	*All Tomorrow's Parties*	Heaven and Hell, vol I (v.a.) (UK: Imaginary/USA: Communion, LP/CD, 1991)
Cabaret Voltaire	*Here She Comes Now*	Extended Play (Rough Trade, 7" EP, 1978)
Cabaret Voltaire	*Here She Comes Now*	Live at YMCA 27-10-79 (Rough Trade, LP, 1979)
Cabaret Voltaire	*Here She Comes Now*	Live (LP, 1980)
Cabaret Voltaire	*The Black Angel's Death Song*	(12")
Cale, John	*I'm Waiting for the Man*	Comes Alive (Ze/Island, LP, 1984)
Captain Pepper & The Legendary Hearts	*Sunday Morning*	Andy Warhol (v.a.) (Sub-Up, LP/CD, 1987)
Carnival of Fools	*Femme Fatale*	(Trimestrale, 7" EP, 1989, w/ bootleg VU lyric book)
Cave, Nick & The Bad Seeds	*All Tomorrow's Parties*	Kicking Against the Pricks (Mute, LP, 1986)
Celibate Rifles, The	*I'm Waiting for the Man*	(Hot, 45 b-side)
Chainsaw	*What Goes On*	Romantik (EP)

ARTIST	VU SONG COVERED	LOCATION (RECORD LABEL, FORMAT, DATE)
Chainsaw	*What Goes On*	(45, 1986)
Chapterhouse	*Lady Godiva's Operation*	Heaven and Hell, vol I (v.a.) (UK: Imaginary/USA: Communion, LP/CD, 1991)
Clock DVA	*The Black Angel's Death Song*	Breakdown (Polydor, 12" EP, 1983)
Color Moves	*Venus in Furs*	Andy Warhol (v.a.) (Sub-Up, LP/CD, 1987)
Comic Spoilers	*All Tomorrow's Parties*	Andy Warhol (v.a.) (Sub-Up, LP/CD, 1987)
Comite Cesne	*Rock & Roll*	Tres Canciones de Lou Reed (Intermitente, 12", 1987)
Comite Cesne	*White Light/White Heat*	Tres Canciones de Lou Reed (Intermitente, 12", 1987)
Company of State	*Venus in Furs*	Still in the Flesh (EP, 1984)
Count, The	*Foggy Notion*	I'm A Star (Flamingo, LP, 1978)
Count, The	*Foggy Notion*	Another View (Varulven, 12" EP, 1985)
Cowboy Junkies	*Sweet Jane*	The Trinity Sessions (RCA, LP/CD, 1988)
Crawdaddys, The	*There She Goes Again*	There She Goes/Why Don't You Smile Now (Voxx/Bomp!, 45, 1980)
Daho, Etianne	*Sunday Morning*	Les Enfants du Velvet (v.a.) (Virgin, EP, 1985)
Derribos Arias	*Lonesome Cowboy Bill*	(LP, 1983)
Desperados	*I'm Waiting for the Man*	(45 b-side, 1987)
Detroit	*Rock & Roll*	Detroit (Paramount, LP, 1971)

ARTIST	VU SONG COVERED	LOCATION (RECORD LABEL, FORMAT, DATE)
Detroit	*Rock & Roll*	(Paramount, 45, 1971)
Dictators, The	*What Goes On*	Fuck 'em If They Can't Take A Joke (ROIR, Cass,1981)
Die Hornissen	*Pale Blue Eyes*	(Paradoxx, 45, 1982)
Dockhuset	*All Tomorrow's Parties*	En Samling Rock Fran Sundsvall (LP, 1985)
Dogs D'Amour	*Heroin*	I Don't Want You to Go (China Records, EP, 1988)
Dolly, Rachel (w/ C. Harper)	*Femme Fatale*	Stolen Property (Flicknife, LP, 1981)
Dr. Mix & The Remix	*Sister Ray*	Wall of Noise (Rough Trade, LP, 1979)
Dragon	*White Light/White Heat*	Recorded Highlights of the Nightmovers Concerts (2LP, 1971)
Dramarama	*Femme Fatale*	Comedy (? Records, EP, 1985)
Droogs	*I'm Waiting for the Man*	Change Is Gonna Come/I'm Waiting For The Man (Plug N Socket, 45)
Dylans, The	*Who Loves the Sun*	Heaven and Hell, vol III (v.a.) (Imaginary, LP/CD/Cass., 1992)
Earth Dies Burning	*Heroin*	Earth Dies Burning (Cass, 1983)
Earthquake	*Head Held High*	Rocking The World (Beserkley, LP, 1975)
Earthquake	*Head Held High*	Live 1975 (UA/Beserkley, LP, 1975)

Artist	VU Song Covered	Location (Record Label, Format, Date)
Eater	*I'm Waiting for the Man*	Eater (The Label, LP)
Eater	*Sweet Jane*	Eater (The Label, LP)
Echo & The Bunnymen	*Run Run Run*	Bedbugs & Ballyhoo (Sire, 12" EP, 1988)
Echo & The Bunnymen	*Foggy Notion*	Heaven and Hell, vol II (v.a.) (Imaginary, LP/CD/Cass., 1991)
Eleventh Dream Day	*Ocean*	Heaven and Hell, vol III (v.a.) (Imaginary, LP/CD/Cass., 1992)
End, The	*Foggy Notion*	The End (Hot Records, LP, 1983)
Erickson, Roky & Evil Hook Wildlife	*Heroin*	The Beast/Heroin (One Big Guitar Records, 12" EP, 1986)
Erickson, Roky & The Explosives	*Heroin*	Gremlins Have Pictures (Pink Dust, LP, 1986)
Falling Spikes	*I'll Be Your Mirror*	Andy Warhol (LP/CD)
Badgemen	*Sister Ray*	Heaven and Hell, vol III (v.a.) (Imaginary, LP/CD/Cass., 1992)
Feelies, The	*What Goes On*	Only Life (LP/CD, 1989)
Ferry, Bryan	*What Goes On*	The Bride Stripped Bare (Polydor, LP/45, 1978)
Flesh & Bones	*Inside Your Heart*	Inside Your Heart (45, 1986)

ARTIST	VU SONG COVERED	LOCATION (RECORD LABEL, FORMAT, DATE)
Flying Klassenfeind	*Venus in Furs*	(Line, 12", 1982)
Forsta Timmarna	*Afterhours*	Tant Strul (45)
Franciose and the Bloomers	*Run Run Run*	Andy Warhol (v.a.) (Sub-Up, LP/CD, 1987)
Gardiner, Paul	*Venus in Furs*	(45/12", 1984)
Ghosts Before Breakfast	*Femme Fatale*	Knapsack Day Dreams (Cass.)
Goddard, Vic & Subway Sect	*Head Held High*	A Retrospective (LP)
Gravity Pirates	*Femme Fatale*	New Age Dreams (Survival Records, LP, 1987)
Great Impostors	*I'm Waiting for the Man*	Dollars In Drag: A Tribute To David Bowie (Pied Piper, LP, 1977)
Green on Red	*There She Goes Again*	(LP)
Guduldig, Bruce & Peter Principle	*Ocean*	Fuck Your Dreams, This Is Heaven (Crammed Discs, LP, 1986)
Half Japanese	*European Son*	Our Solar System (Iridesence, LP, 1984)
Half Japanese	*Foggy Notion*	Half Gentlemen, Not Beasts (Armageddon, 3LP, 1980)
Half Japanese	*I Can't Stand It*	Half Gentlemen, Not Beasts (Armageddon, 3LP, 1980)
Half Japanese	*I Heard Her Call My Name*	Heaven and Hell, vol III (v.a.) (Imaginary, LP/CD/Cass., 1992)

Artist	VU Song Covered	Location (Record Label, Format, Date)
Hanover Fist	*Femme Fatale*	Hanover Fist (Capitol, 12" EP)
Harper, Charlie	*I'm Waiting for the Man*	Stolen Property (Flicknife, LP, 1981)
Harvey, Tina	*I'm Waiting for the Man*	(45, 1976)
Hayes, J.M.	*Sunday Morning*	Bum (Cass.)
Hayes, J.M., & Fred Johnson	*Jesus*	Sparkles From the Wheel (Cass.)
Heart of Juliet Jones, The	*White Light/White Heat*	(Poko, 45, 1985)
Hellzephyrs	*Sweet Jane*	Kalabalik (Sonet, LP, 1983)
Hidden Charms	*Guess I'm Falling in Love*	Hidden Charms (LP, 1985)
Hitmakers	*I'll Be Your Mirror*	(LP, 1977)
Hurrah!	*Sweet Jane*	Heaven and Hell, vol II (v.a.) (Imaginary, LP/CD/Cass., 1991)
Imperial Dogs	*I'm Waiting for the Man*	I'm Waiting For The Man (Back Door Man, 45, 1975)
Inside Out	*I'm Waiting for the Man*	Andy Warhol (v.a.) (Sub-Up, LP/CD, 1987)
Into Paradise	*Beginning to See the Light*	Heaven and Hell, vol III (v.a.) (Imaginary, LP/CD/Cass., 1992)
James	*Sunday Morning*	Heaven and Hell, vol I (v.a.) (UK: Imaginary/ USA: Communion, LP/CD, 1991)
Jane's Addiction	*Rock & Roll*	Jane's Addiction Live (XXX, LP, 1987)

ARTIST	VU SONG COVERED	LOCATION (RECORD LABEL, FORMAT, DATE)
Japan	*All Tomorrow's Parties*	Quiet Life (Ariola, LP, 1979)
Japan	*All Tomorrow's Parties*	(Ariola Hansa, 12", 1981)
Japan	*All Tomorrow's Parties*	Assemblage (Ariola Hansa, LP, 1982)
Jazz Butcher, The	*Sweet Jane*	Marine (EP)
Jazz Butcher, The	*Sweet Jane*	Hamburg (LP, 1985)
Jellyfishbabies	*Here She Comes Now*	Here She Comes Now (45, 1989)
Jellyfish Kiss	*I'm Sticking With You*	Heaven and Hell, vol III (v.a.) (Imaginary, LP/CD/Cass., 1992)
Jeremy's Secret	*Some Kinda Love*	The Snowball Effect (Deep 6, LP, 1984)
Johnson, Peter C.	*Pale Blue Eyes*	Peter C. Johnson (CBS, LP, 1980)
Joy Division	*Sister Ray*	Still (Factory, 2LP, 1981)
Klau, Nicholas, Steven Brown, Peter Principle	*Venus in Furs*	Fuck Your Dreams, This Is Heaven (Crammed Discs, LP, 1986)
Lamb, Annabelle	*Sweet Jane*	Brides (RCA, LP, 1987)
Leather Nun, The	*Chelsea Girl*	(12" EP, 1985)
Levellers 5	*Some Kinda Love*	Heaven and Hell, vol II (v.a.) (Imaginary, LP/CD/Cass., 1991)

ARTIST	VU SONG COVERED	LOCATION (RECORD LABEL, FORMAT, DATE)
Lime Spiders, The	*I Heard Her Call My Name*	I Heard Her Call My Name/My Favorite Room (Virgin, 12", 1984)
Little Wretches, The	*I'll Be Your Mirror*	Just Another Nail In My Coffin (Bamm! Bamm!, CD, 1990)
Little Wretches, The	*What Goes On*	Just About Due/What Goes On (Get Hip, 45, 1988)
Lloyd, Claudia	*Femme Fatale*	Mission is Terminated (Nice, 2LP, 1983)
Lone Justice	*Sweet Jane*	I Found Love (Geffen, EP, 1987)
Long Ryders, The	*What Goes On*	Metallic B.O. (Cass., 1989)
Mansions, Fatima	*Lady Godiva's Operation*	Heaven and Hell, vol II (v.a.) (Imaginary, LP/CD/Cass., 1991)
Marquis de Sade	*White Light/White Heat*	Dantzig Twist (EMI/Pathe, LP, 1980)
Method Actors	*All Tomorrow's Parties*	Luxury (LP, 1984)
Mistaken, The	*I'm Set Free*	The Mistaken (Bad Trio, LP, 1988)
Mitsouko, Rita	*All Tomorrow's Parties*	Les Enfants Du Velvet (v.a.) (Virgin, EP/CD, 1985)
Mock Turtles, The	*Pale Blue Eyes*	Heaven and Hell, vol II (v.a.) (Imaginary, LP/CD/Cass., 1991)
Moore, Thurston	*European Son*	The End of Music As We Know It (ROIR, Cass, 1988)
Mother's Ruin	*Rock & Roll*	Mother's Ruin (LP, 1981)

ARTIST	VU SONG COVERED	LOCATION (RECORD LABEL, FORMAT, DATE)
Motorcycle Boy	*Run Run Run*	Heaven and Hell, vol I (v.a.) (UK: Imaginary / USA: Communion, LP/CD, 1991)
Mott The Hoople	*Sweet Jane*	All The Young Dudes (Columbia, LP/CD)
MX-80	*The Gift*	Hard Attack (LP)
Nelson, Bill	*Lonesome Cowboy Bill*	Heaven and Hell, vol II (v.a.) (Imaginary, LP/CD/Cass., 1991)
New Fast Automatic Daffodils	*I'm Set Free*	Heaven and Hell, vol III (v.a.) (Imaginary, LP/CD/Cass., 1992)
New Order	*Sister Ray*	Like A Girl, I Want You To Keep Coming (v.a.) (Giorno Poetry Systems, LP/CD, 1989)
Nico	*All Tomorrow's Parties*	European Diary – Live (ROIR–USA, Cass., 1983)
Nico	*All Tomorrow's Parties*	Behind The Iron Curtain (Castle Comm. 2LP/CD, '86)
Nico	*All Tomorrow's Parties*	Live In Tokyo (Castle Comm., LP/CD, 1987)
Nico	*All Tomorrow's Parties*	Blue Angel (Aura Records, LP/CD/Cass., 1986)
Nico	*Femme Fatale*	Blue Angel (Aura Records, LP/CD/Cass., 1986)
Nico	*Femme Fatale*	Procession (1/2 Records, 12" EP, 1982)
Nico	*Femme Fatale*	European Diary 1982 (1/2 Records, Cass, 1983)
Nico	*Femme Fatale*	Live Heroes (Performance Records, 12"EP, 1986)

Artist	VU Song Covered	Location (Record Label, Format, Date)
Nico	*Femme Fatale*	Live In Tokyo (Castle Comm. Records, LP/CD, 1987)
Nico	*Femme Fatale*	Behind The Iron Curtain (Castle Comm, 2LP/CD, '86)
Nico	*I'm Waiting for the Man*	Ziggy (12" EP, 1982)
Nico	*Here She Comes Now*	Nig Heist (LP)
Nig Heist	*Here She Comes Now*	Heaven and Hell, vol I (v.a.) (UK: Imaginary/USA: Communion, LP/CD, 1991)
Nirvana		
No Italinna Huraa!	*Afterhours*	Hulalalaa (Pygmi/Bonita Beat, LP, 1986)
No More	*I'm Waiting for the Man*	Different Longings (12" EP, 1986)
OMD	*I'm Waiting for the Man*	Messages (Dindisc, 10" EP, 1980)
Original Sins, The	*Head Held High*	Heaven and Hell, vol III (v.a.) (Imaginary, LP/CD/Cass., 1992)
Orphan, Shelleyan	*Who Loves the Sun*	Heaven and Hell, vol II (v.a.) (Imaginary, LP/CD/Cass., 1991)
Pantano Boas, The	*Heroin*	Full Blood Crash (3 Cipreses, LP, 1987)
Pantano Boas, The	*Sister Ray*	Full Blood Crash (3 Cipreses, LP, 1987)
Pantino Boas, The	*I'm Waiting for the Man*	Full Blood Crash (3 Cipreses, LP, 1987)
Pickett, Charlie & The Eggs	*Lonesome Cowboy Bill*	Live At The Button (Open, LP, 1981)
Pinheads, The	*Sweet Jane*	Rotn/Roll/Live (Garageland, LP, 1985)

Artist	VU Song Covered	Location (Record Label, Format, Date)
Pinheads, The	*Sweet Jane*	Original Soundtrack from 'Out of Focus' (Garageland, LP, 1983)
Pinheads, The	*Venus in Furs*	Original Soundtrack from 'Out of Focus' (Garageland, LP, 1983)
Pinky Silence & The Mad Horses	*European Son*	Andy Warhol (v.a.) (Sub-Up, LP/CD, 1987)
Plain Jane & The Jokes	*What Goes On*	The Joke's On You (Sick Sound, LP, 1981)
Pleasure Heads	*Foggy Notion*	Catholic Guilt/Foggy Notion (Cubist Productions, 45, 1990)
Primatives, The	*I'll Be Your Mirror*	Purity (RCA, LP, 1989)
Professionals, The	*White Light/White Heat*	1-2-3 (Virgin, 45)
Propaganda	*Femme Fatale*	The 9 Lives of Dr. Mabuse (ZTT, 12" EP, 1984)
Psychic TV	*Sunday Morning*	NY Scum (LP, 198?)
Pulnoc	*All Tomorrow's Parties*	City of Hysteria (Arista, CD, 1991)
Pussy Galore	*Heroin*	Exile On Main Street (Cass.)
Quinn, Paul & Edwyn Collins	*Pale Blue Eyes*	(Swamplands, 12"/45, 1984)
Rainy Day	*I'll Be Your Mirror*	Rainy Day (Rough Trade, LP/CD, 1984)

Artist	VU Song Covered	Location (Record Label, Format, Date)
Ranaldo, Lee	*Stephanie Says*	Heaven and Hell, vol III (v.a.) (Imaginary, LP/CD/Cass., 1992)
Reed, Lou	*A Sheltered Life*	Rock & Roll Heart (Arista, LP, 1976)
Reed, Lou	*Andy's Chest*	Transformer (RCA, LP, 1972)
Reed, Lou	*Heroin*	Rock'n'Roll Animal (RCA, LP, 1974)
Reed, Lou	*Heroin*	Live In Italy (RCA, 2LP, 1984)
Reed, Lou	*I Can't Stand It*	Lou Reed (RCA, LP, 1972)
Reed, Lou	*I'm Waiting for the Man*	Live (RCA, LP, 1975)
Reed, Lou	*I'm Waiting for the Man*	Take No Prisoners (Arista, 2LP, 1978)
Reed, Lou	*I'm Waiting for the Man*	Live In Italy (RCA, 2LP, 1984)
Reed, Lou	*Lisa Says*	Lou Reed (RCA, LP, 1971)
Reed, Lou	*Ocean*	Lou Reed (RCA, LP, 1971)
Reed, Lou	*Oh Jim*	Berlin (RCA, LP, 1973)
Reed, Lou	*Oh Jim*	Live (RCA, LP, 1975)
Reed, Lou	*Pale Blue Eyes*	Take No Prisoners (Arista, 2LP, 1978)
Reed, Lou	*Real Good Time Together*	Street Hassle (Arista, LP, 1978)
Reed, Lou	*Ride Into the Sun*	Lou Reed (RCA, LP, 1971)
Reed, Lou	*Rock & Roll*	Rock'n'Roll Animal (RCA, LP, 1974)

Artist	VU Song Covered	Location (Record Label, Format, Date)
Reed, Lou	*Rock & Roll*	Live In Italy (RCA, 2LP, 1984)
Reed, Lou	*Sad Song*	Berlin (RCA, LP, 1973)
Reed, Lou	*Sad Song*	Live (RCA, LP, 1975)
Reed, Lou	*She's My Best Friend*	Coney Island Baby (RCA, LP/CD, 1976)
Reed, Lou	*Sister Ray*	Live In Italy (RCA, 2LP, 1984)
Reed, Lou	*Some Kinda Love*	Live In Italy (RCA, 2LP, 1984)
Reed, Lou	*Sweet Jane*	Rock'n'Roll Animal (RCA, LP, 1974)
Reed, Lou	*Sweet Jane*	Take No Prisoners (Arista, 2LP, 1978)
Reed, Lou	*Sweet Jane*	Live In Italy (RCA, 2LP, 1984)
Reed, Lou	*Walk and Talk It*	Lou Reed (RCA, LP, 1971)
Reed, Lou	*White Light/White Heat*	Rock'n'Roll Animal (RCA, LP, 1974)
Reed, Lou	*White Light/White Heat*	Live In Italy (RCA, 2LP, 1984)
Reegs, The	*All Tomorrow's Parties*	Heaven and Hell, vol II (v.a.) (Imaginary, LP/CD/Cass., 1991)
R.E.M.	*Afterhours*	Losing My Religion B-side (Warner, CD/12" EP, 1991)
R.E.M.	*Femme Fatale*	Dead Letter Office (IRS Records, LP/CD, 1987)
R.E.M.	*Femme Fatale*	Superman (IRS Records, 12")
R.E.M.	*Pale Blue Eyes*	(12", 1984)

ARTIST	VU SONG COVERED	LOCATION (RECORD LABEL, FORMAT, DATE)
R.E.M.	*There She Goes Again*	(IRS, 45, 1983)
R.E.M.	*There She Goes Again*	(The Bob Magazine, flexi 7", 1986)
Revenge	*White Light/White Heat*	Heaven and Hell, vol II (v.a.) (Imaginary, LP/CD/Cass., 1991)
Riats, The	*Run Run Run*	Sunday Morning/Run Run Run (Omega, 45, 1967)
Riats, The	*Sunday Morning*	Sunday Morning/Run Run Run (Omega, 45, 1967)
Ride	*European Son*	Heaven and Hell, vol I (v.a.) (UK: Imaginary/USA: Communion, LP/CD, 1991)
Robichaud, Edward	*Rock & Roll*	(Pop Tone, 45, 1981)
Rollins, Henry	*Move Right In*	Hot Animal Machine (Texas Hotel, LP, 1986)
Rollins, Henry	*Move Right In*	Do It (Texas Hotel, LP, 1988)
Ronson, Mick	*White Light/White Heat*	Play, Don't Worry (RCA, LP, 1975)
Roosters	*Femme Fatale*	Japan (LP)
Roper, Skid & Mojo Nixon	*Sister Ray*	(Enigma, LP)
Royhka, Kauko (Carl Bold)	*Lady Godiva's Operation*	Steppaillen (Mirror, LP, 1980)
Runaways, The	*Rock & Roll*	The Runaways (Mercury, LP, 1976)
Runaways, The	*Rock & Roll*	Live In Japan (Mercury, LP, 1977)
Russell, Charles	*All Tomorrow's Parties*	Charles Russell (Jargon, LP, 1987)

Artist	VU Song Covered	Location (Record Label, Format, Date)
Russell, Charles	*All Tomorrow's Parties*	All Tomorrow's Parties (Jargon, 45)
Ryder, Mitch	*Rock & Roll*	We Love You, Of Course We Do (12")
Sacred Cowboys, The	*Run Run Run*	(Manmade Records, LP, 1984)
Scooters	*Sweet Jane*	Commando (v.a.) (Skydog, LP/CD, 197?)
Scott, Jeff & Josef Marc	*I'll Be Your Mirror*	America's Newest Hitmakers (Mirror, EP)
Screaming Trees	*What Goes On*	Heaven and Hell, vol I (v.a.) (UK: Imaginary / USA: Communion, LP/CD, 1991)
Screaming Tribesmen	*I Can't Stand It*	(12" EP, 1989)
Se	*What Goes On*	Nyt (Love, 45, 1978)
Seberg, Marc	*Venus in Furs*	Les Enfants du Velvet (v.a.) (Virgin, EP, 1985)
Shades, Phil	*Rock & Roll*	Phil Shades (Wampum, LP, 1978)
Sister Rain	*Sister Ray*	Sister Rain (Voices of Wonder, LP, 1988)
Sisters of Mercy	*Sister Ray*	Spirits/Sister Ray (Candelmass Records, 45, 1985)
Skat	*Femme Fatale*	(Graduate, 45)
Slaughter & The Dogs	*I'm Waiting for the Man*	Do It Dog Style (Decca, LP, 1978)
Slits, The	*Sister Ray*	(Y, LP, 1978)
Smith, Kendra	*All Tomorrow's Parties*	All Morgen's Parties (The Bob Magazine, flexi 7", '87)

Artist	VU Song Covered	Location (Record Label, Format, Date)
Spy vs. Spy	*Venus in Furs*	Tape Report: The Best of Paul K & The Weathermen (Shrunken Stomach, Cass., 1987)
Stitching Brown Underwear	*Afterhours*	Sammy Sou, How Do You Do (Cass., 1987)
Strawberry Switchblade	*Sunday Morning*	(Korona, 12", 1984)
Suicide	*Sister Ray*	Suicide (Ze/Antilles, LP, 1980)
Suicide	*Sister Ray*	Half Alive (ROIR, Cass.)
Sunset Strip, The	*Move Right In*	Move Right In (Au Go-Go, LP, 1991)
Superlovers	*Femme Fatale*	Andy Warhol (v.a.) (Sub-Up, LP/CD, 1987)
Surrealists	*Pale Blue Eyes*	Where's Dada (Vagrant, EP, 1989)
Sweet, Rachel	*New Age*	Protect The Innocent (Stiff, LP, 1980)
Swervedriver	*Jesus*	Heaven and Hell, vol III (v.a.) (Imaginary, LP/CD/Cass., 1992)
Tabor, June	*All Tomorrow's Parties*	(LP, 1990)
Taxi Girl	*Stephanie Says*	Les Enfants du Velvet (v.a.) (Virgin, EP, 1985)
Telescopes, The	*Candy Says*	Heaven and Hell, vol I (v.a.) (UK: Imaginary / USA: Communion, LP/CD, 1991)
Terrell, Aliss	*I'll Be Your Mirror*	Les Enfants Du Velvet (v.a.) (Virgin, EP, 1985)
Third Rail	*Sweet Jane*	(Rat, 45, 1977)

ARTIST	VU SONG COVERED	LOCATION (RECORD LABEL, FORMAT, DATE)
Thorne, Tracey	*Femme Fatale*	Femme Fatale (Cherry Red, LP, 1985)
Tom Tom Club	*Femme Fatale*	Boom Boom Chi Boom Boom (Fontana, LP, 1988)
Torme, Berne	*Chelsea Girl*	Turn Out The Lights (Kamalage, 2LP, 1981)
Trockener Kecks	*Femme Fatale*	Schliessbaum (LP, 1981)
True Believers	*Foggy Notion*	It's Hard To Be Cool In An Uncool World (I Wanna, LP, 1988)
True Believers	*Train 'Round the Bend*	True Believers (EMI/Rounder, LP, 1986)
Tucker, Moe	*Guess I'm Falling in Love*	MOEJADKATEBARRY (50,000,000,000,000,000,000,-000 WATTS, 12" EP, 1987)
Tucker, Moe	*Heroin*	Playing Possum (Trash Records, LP, 1982)
Tucker, Moe	*Hey Mr. Rain*	MOEJADKATEBARRY (50,000,000,000,000,000,000,-000 WATTS, 12" EP, 1986)
Tucker, Moe	*I'm Sticking With You*	I'm Sticking With You (Varulven, 45, 1980)
Tucker, Moe	*I'm Sticking With You*	Another View (Varulven, 12" EP, 1986)
Tucker, Moe	*Pale Blue Eyes*	Life In Exile After Abdication (50,000,000,000,-000,000,000 WATTS, LP/CD, 1989)
Tucker, Moe	*I'm Waiting for the Man*	I Spent a Week There the Other Night (New Rose, CD/Cass., 1992)

Artist	VU Song Covered	Location (Record Label, Format, Date)
Twiggy and the Aliens	*There She Goes Again*	Andy Warhol (v.a.) (Sub-Up, LP/CD, 1987)
Two Nice Girls	*Sweet Jane*	Two Nice Girls (Rough Trade, LP/CD, 1989)
UK Subs	*I'm Waiting for the Man*	I'm Waiting For The Man (45)
Unlimited Systems	*Pale Blue Eyes*	Half-Broken Hearted (Schnick Schnick, LP, 1985)
Voice of the Beehive	*Jesus*	I Say Nothing/Jesus (12")
Wasps, The	*I'm Waiting for the Man*	Live At The Vortex (NEMS, LP, 1977)
Wasted Youth	*Real Good Time Together*	Beginning of the End (LP, 1982)
Watermelon Men	*There She Goes Again*	Past, Present and Future (What Goes On, LP, 1985)
We Free Kings	*Run Run Run*	Still Standing (DDT, EP, 1987)
Wedding Present, The	*She's My Best Friend*	Heaven and Hell, vol I (v.a.) (UK: Imaginary/ USA: Communion, LP/CD, 1991)
Well, The	*Rock & Roll*	The Well (Cass.)
Widowed Isis	*White Light/White Heat*	Widowed Isis (Zed, EP, 1987)
Yardbirds, The	*I'm Waiting for the Man*	Last Rave Up In L.A. (3LP, 1980)
Yo La Tengo	*It's All Right (The Way That You Live)*	New Wave Hot Dogs (Coyote, LP/CD, 1987)

In addition, the following artists are known to have included cover versions of Velvet Underground songs in their live sets at one time or another: **The Angry Samoans:** That's the Story of My Life. **Bauhaus:** I'm Waiting for the Man. **Phil Boa:** I'm Waiting for the Man. **Victor Bockris (NYC, 1982):** The Gift. **David Bowie:** Sweet Jane; White Light/White Heat. **Jim Carroll:** Sweet Jane. **The Cars:** Here She Comes Now; I'm Waiting for the Man. **The Darling Buds:** There She Goes Again. **The Dolly Mixtures:** Femme Fatale. **Echo & the Bunnymen:** Here She Comes Now; Heroin; Rock & Roll; Sister Ray; There She Goes Again; What Goes On. **Roky Erickson & the Aliens:** Heroin. **The Feelies:** European Son; Run Run Run; Sweet Jane; Real Good Time Together. **Flesh for Lulu:** Sister Ray; Femme Fatale; Rock & Roll. **Gang of Four:** Sweet Jane. **Vic Godard & Subway Sect:** Head Held High. **Half Japanese:** Femme Fatale; Lonesome Cowboy Bill; Sweet Jane; What Goes On; White Light/White Heat. **Debby Harry:** I'm Waiting for the Man. **House of Love:** I Can't Stand It. **Hüsker Du:** Sweet Jane. **The Jazz Butcher:** I'm Waiting for the Man; Sweet Jane. **Greg Kihn Band:** Rock & Roll; Sweet Jane. **Daniel Lanios:** I'm Waiting for the Man. **Lenny Kaye Connection:** I'm Set Free. **Richard Lloyd:** I'm Waiting for the Man. **Lone Justice:** Head Held High; Sweet Jane. **The Long Ryders:** Pale Blue Eyes; Run Run Run; White Light/White Heat. **Motorhead:** I'm Waiting for the Man. **New Order:** Sister Ray. **Paris 1942:** Heroin; Pale Blue Eyes; White Light/White Heat. **Pere Ubu:** Heroin; Pale Blue Eyes. **The Pink Fairies:** I'm Waiting for the Man. **Plastic People of the Universe (Prague):** Afterhours; Beginning to See the Light; Candy Says; Here She Comes Now; I'm Waiting for the Man; Pale Blue Eyes; Rock & Roll; Sister Ray; Sunday Morning; Sweet Jane; What Goes On; Who Loves the Sun. **Iggy Pop:** I'm Waiting for the Man. **Pulnoc (Prague):** All Tomorrow's Parties; Lady Godiva's Operation. **Tom Robinson Band:** I'm Waiting for the Man. **Simple Minds:** White Light/White Heat. **Sisters of Mercy:** Sister Ray. **The Skids:** What Goes On. **The Slits:** Femme Fatale. **Patti Smith:** I'm Waiting for the Man. **The Triffids:** Beginning to See the Light; Femme Fatale; I'm Waiting for the Man; Inside Your Heart; Pale Blue Eyes; Sweet Jane; There She Goes Again; What Goes On. **The Tubes:** I'm Waiting for the Man. **TV Personalities:** I'm Waiting for the Man.

FILM

Velvet Underground Films

Venus In Furs
(1965, 6 min, color)
Director: Piero Heliczer
Featuring: Lou Reed, John Cale, Angus MacLise, Barbara Rubin
Music: The Velvet Underground, including **Heroin** and **Venus In Furs** live from the CBS news broadcast with Heliczer on sax.
Availability: not known

Andy Warhol's Exploding Plastic Inevitable
(August 1966, 22 min, color and b&w)
Director: Ronald Nameth
Featuring: The Velvet Underground, Gerard Malanga, Mary Woronov
Music: The Velvet Underground, Nico. Music from the **VU & Nico** LP and Nico's **Chelsea Girl**, except for two live songs by the VU lineup in this film: Cale – vcl, kybds; Morrison – gtr; Tucker – bass; MacLise – tablas. (Reed was sick in hospital.)
Availability: Available for rent from the New York City Filmaker's Cooperative.
Of note: An impressionistic view of an EPI performance.

Hedy
(November 1965, 70 min, b&w)
Director: Andy Warhol
Featuring: Mario Montez, Mary Woronov, Gerard Malanga, Jack Smith
Music: John Cale and Lou Reed
Availability: Rarely shown. Available for rent from the New York City Filmaker's Cooperative.
Of note: Camp portrayal of Hedy Lamarr's shoplifting trial.

Mary For Mary
(1966, 16 min, b&w)
Director: Gerard Malanga
Featuring: Mary Woronov
Music: The Velvet Underground
Availability: Not known

More Milk Yvette
(November 1965)
Director: Andy Warhol
Featuring: Mario Montez
Music: The Velvet Underground
Availability: Rarely shown. Available for rent from the New York City Filmaker's Cooperative.

The Chelsea Girls
(Summer 1966, 210 min, color and b&w)
Director: Andy Warhol
Featuring: Ondine, Nico, Brigid Polk, Mary Woronov, Eric Emerson, International Velvet, Ingrid Superstar, Gerard Malanga and Marie Menken
Music: The Velvet Underground
Availability: Rarely shown. Available for rent from the New York City Filmaker's Cooperative.
Of note: 1. A room-by-room exploration of the infamous Chelsea Hotel and the denizens to be found therein.
2. The film known as 'The Gerard Malanga Story' is a 70 minute excerpt from 'The Chelsea Girls' and it is this portion which includes the VU music.

The Velvet Underground & Nico (A Symphony of Sound)
(January 1966, 70 min, b&w)
Director: Andy Warhol
Featuring: The Velvet Underground & Nico
Music: The Velvet Underground & Nico
Availability: Rarely shown. Available for rent from the New York City Filmaker's Cooperative.
Of note: The VU & Nico perform a long, improvised piece in the Factory. The police arrive twice to quiet the din. They succeed and most of the rest of the film is a fixed-camera look at the band milling about.

Diaries, Notes And Sketches
(1965-1970, color)
Director: Jonas Mekas
Featuring: Andy Warhol, Jonas Mekas, The Velvet Underground, Nico, Gerard Malanga, Mario Montez, Jack Smith, Naomi Levine, Barbara Rubin, Yoko Ono
Music: The Velvet Underground, Nico. Some studio songs, but most is great VU improvisation.
Availability: Rarely shown. Available for rent from the New York City Filmaker's Cooperative.
Of note: 1. An assemblage of home-movie-style clips featuring Mekas and famous friends from the New York scene.
2. The VU are shown briefly, playing at the 1966 Psychiatrists Convention (*sic*), and heard for approximately 20 minutes throughout the film.
3. Clips from the film were used in Nico's 1991 video 'Frozen Warnings'.

Velvet Underground
Television Appearances

The Making of an Underground Film
Date: Filmed November 1965, shown December 1965
Channel: CBS-TV
Songs: Heroin, Venus In Furs
Of note: Filmed during the making of Piero Heliczer's "Venus In Furs." Sterling, John and Lou play with shirts off, in body paint, with director Heliczer joining in on saxophone.

USA Artists
Date: February 1966
Channel: WNET (NY)
Songs: Venus In Furs, Heroin
Of note: The show is about Warhol, on the eve of the EPI. He introduces the VU: "I'm sponsoring a new band. It's called the Velvet Underground. Since I don't really believe in painting anymore, I thought it would be a nice way of combining music, art and films all together. The whole thing's being auditioned tomorrow at nine o'clock. If it works out, it might be very glamorous."

Upbeat
Date: 8 January 1967, 15 July 1967
Channel: Local TV show (Cleveland, Ohio)
Songs: Guess I'm Falling In Love
Of note: Cleveland TV Guide listing for 8 January 1967: "Upbeat – with Marvin Gaye & Tammie Terrell, The Music Explosion, Velvet Underground, 5th Estate and Donna Sears."

Lou Reed, John Cale, Nico – Live
Date: 29 January 1972
Channel: French TV
Songs: I'm Waiting For The Man, Berlin, The Black Angel's Death Song, Wild Child, Empty Bottles, Heroin, Ghost Story, The Biggest, Loudest, Heaviest Group of All, Femme Fatale, I'll Be Your Mirror, All Tomorrow's Parties, Janitor of Lunacy
Of note: 1. Filmed at the Bataclan Club in Paris and rebroadcast in a shortened version at least once.
2. The French government now controls this film, and despite the best efforts of the BBC, Warner Brothers, PolyGram and the Foundation Cartier, too high a price is being asked for it to be released in its entirety. Short clips were included in the 'Southbank' and 'Arsenal' TV shows.

Pop Deux
Date: 10 June 1972
Channel: TF 1 (France)
Songs: I'm Waiting For The Man, Wild Child, Femme Fatale, I'll Be Your Mirror
Of note: 1. French critics discuss the VU, Lou, John, Nico, and the state of rock.
2. Includes four songs from the Bataclan show. There is some evidence to suggest that this may now be the only remnant of the Bataclan TV show in the French TV archives.

Arsenal
Date: Filmed September 1985 through May 1986, shown 19 May 1986
Channel: Catalonian TV3 (Spain)
Songs: Loop, The Ostrich and other rarities
Of note: 1. Impressionistic VU history, punctuated by 1985 interview with Sterling and film of him overdubbing guitar onto a 1984 performance by Cale of **I'm Waiting for the Man**.
2. The soundtrack is made up of rare and live material.

South Bank Show
Date: Filmed September 1985, shown 27 April 1986
Channel: London Weekend Television
Songs: Thoughtless Kind (Cale), Femme Fatale (Nico)
Of note: 1. Documentary with 1985 interviews with Lou, John, Nico, Sterling, Maureen, plus Gerard Malanga, Victor Bockris, Robert Christgau.
2. Includes clips from the Paris 1972 show (see entry).

Films of Related Interest

Dirt
(12 min, color and b&w)
Director: Piero Heliczer
Featuring: Andy Warhol, Angus MacLise

Invasion of The Thunderbolt People
Director: Ira Cohen
Featuring: Tony and Beverly Conrad, Harvey Cohen
Music: Angus and Hettie MacLise

The Soap Opera
(13 min)
Director: Piero Heliczer
Featuring: Piero Heliczer, Jack Smith, LaMonte Young, Marian Zazeela, Angus MacLise
Of note: Also exists in a 70 minute version.

Flaming Creatures
(1963)
Director: Jack Smith
Featuring: Mario Montez
Music: LaMonte Young, Marian Zazeela, Billy Name and Angus MacLise, engineered by Tony Conrad

Normal Love
(1963)
Director: Jack Smith
Featuring: Andy Warhol, Gerard Malanga, Angus MacLise, Tiny Tim

Chumlum
(1964, 30 min)
Director: Ron Rice
Featuring: Jack Smith, Tiny Tim, Gerard Malanga
Music: Angus MacLise

The Autumn Feast
(1964)
Director: Piero Heliczer
Music: Angus MacLise, Tony Conrad, Piero Heliczer

Satisfaction
(1965, 10 min, color and b&w)
Director: Piero Heliczer
Featuring: Angus MacLise

The Closet
(1965)
Director: Andy Warhol
Featuring: Nico, Randy Borscheidt

* * * *
(1967, 1500 min)
Director: Andy Warhol
Featuring: Nico, Viva, Ingrid Superstar, Ultra Violet, Ondine, Edie Sedgwick, Tom Baker
Music: From Nico's **Chelsea Girl** LP
Of note: Like "The Chelsea Girls," this film is divided into several sections. Nico appears in the "High Ashbury" segment, #76.

I, A Man
(July, 1967, 100 min, b&w)
Director: Andy Warhol
Featuring: Nico, Ingrid Superstar, Valerie Solanas, Tom Baker
Of note: This is Solanas' only appearance in a Warhol film.

Joan of Arc
(1967)
Director: Piero Heliczer
Featuring: Jack Smith, Ira Cohen, Gerard Malanga, Angus MacLise

Hymn To The Mystic Fire
(1981)
Director: Sheldon Rochlin
Music: Music in part by Angus MacLise

Ossian: American Boy, Tibetan Monk
(1983-1990, 35 min, color)
Featuring: Ossian and Hettie MacLise
Of Note: 1. Profile of Angus' son Ossian, who was selected at an early age to be a monk in Nepal. Most of the film concerns Ossian's daily life as a 13-year old student monk at age 13 in 1983, with a 1990 update.
2. Available on Home Video through Mystic Arts, USA.

Frozen Warnings
(1966/67, 1991, 4 min, color and b&w)
Director: Stephen Seymour
Featuring: Nico, Andy Warhol, The Velvet Underground, Bob Dylan, Gerard Malanga, Salvador Dali
Music: Nico's Frozen Warnings
Of note: 1. Comprises clips and still photographs well-assembled from many sources – screen tests, shots around the Factory, the VU playing at the 1966 Psychiatrists Convention, etc.

2. The title song is from the CD reissue of Nico's LP **The Marble Index**.
3. Produced by Stephen Seymour and Gerard Malanga.
4. Available from Elektra Entertainment.

Andy Warhol – Superstar
(1989, 90 min, color and b&w)
Director: Chris Workman
Featuring: Andy Warhol, Edie Sedgewick, Holly Woodlawn, Lou Reed et al.
Music: Various and incongruous: Blondie, Vanilla Fudge – no VU.
Availability: Vestron Home Video.
Of note: 1. Archive footage of Andy and the Factory gang, plus recent interviews with the surviving members.
2. Includes extremely rare brief footage of the VU playings Vanilla Fudge. The clips used are of superb quality, but there is no other mention of the band.

PRINT

Velvet Underground and Related Books

Note: The following books are listed alphabetically by author.

Lou Reed: The Life, the Poems, and the Music of a Hero of American Rock
Author: Abate, Anna
(127pp, 1980; Savelli Editori, Milan Italy)
Of note: Text in Italian.

Warhol Films
Author: Abrahams, Anna
(72pp, 1989; Studiecentrum Nederlands Filminstituut, Amsterdam Holland, ISBN: 90-72876-01-6)
Of note: Text in Dutch.

Velvet Underground
Author: Albertoli, Carlo
(96pp, 1989; Stampa Alternativa, Rome Italy)
Of note: Brief VU history in Italian, with accurate Italian/English lyrics; included 7" EP with studio version of the VU performing **Ride into the Sun** (with vocal) plus cover versions of **Femme Fatale** by the Carnival of Fools and **European Son** by Subterranean Dining Rooms. Reprinted in 1991 with a 3" CD single replacing the 7" record.

Il Cinema di Andy Warhol
Author: Apra, Adriano and Enzo Ungari
(116pp, 1972; Film Studio 70)
Of note: Text in Italian.

The Velvet Underground
Author: Arnaiz, Jorge and Jose Luis Mendoza
(288pp, 1989; Catedra, Madrid Spain, ISBN: 84-376-0839-2)
Of note: Basic history of the band, with photographs from Uptight. Accurate Spanish/English lyrics. Text in Spanish.

Delmore Schwartz: The Life of an American Poet
Author: Atlas, James
(418pp, 1977; Farrar Straus & Giroux, New York; Faber & Faber, London)
Of note: Lou Reed studied under Schwartz for a time and has always revered the man and his work.

Psychotic Reactions and Carburetor Dung
Author: Bangs, Lester
(391pp, 1987; Knopf, New York, ISBN: 0-394-53896-X; Heinemann, London, ISBN: 0-434-04456-3. Current: 1990, Minerva, London, ISBN: 0-7493-9095-6)

The New American Cinema
Author: Battcock, Gregory
(256pp, 1967; E. P. Dutton, New York)
Of note: Includes photograph of Nico.

Lou Reed
Author: Binaghi, Walter
(172pp, 1979; Arcana Editrice, Rome Italy)
Of note: Includes poor translations of the lyrics.

The Life and Death of Andy Warhol
Author: Bockris, Victor
(320pp, 1989; Bantam, New York, ISBN: 90-325-0335-9; Muller, London, ISBN: 0-09-172637-9. Current: Penguin, London, ISBN: 0-14-012774-7)

Up-Tight: The Velvet Underground Story
Author: Bockris, Victor and Gerard Malanga
(128pp, 1983; Omnibus, London, ISBN: 0-7119-0168-6)
Of note: Until Sterling Morrison publishes his forthcoming account, this is likely to remain *the* book for VU history, even though the emphasis is much more on 1966-68 than 1969-1970 (when Malanga was no longer part of the troupe), with the best assortment of photographs and quotes to be found anywhere. Editions also published in USA (William Morrow), Germany (Sonnentanz) and Japan (Fool's Mate).

With William Burroughs: A Report From The Bunker
Author: Bockris, Victor and William Burroughs
(250pp, 1981; Seaver Books, New York, ISBN: h/b 0-3945-1809-8, p/b 0-394-17828-9)
Of note: Burroughs' meeting with Lou is recounted here.

Andy Warhol
Author: Bourdon, David
(432pp, 1989; Harry N. Abrams, Inc., New York, ISBN: h/b 0-8109-1761-0, p/b 0-8109-8110-6)
Of note: Includes EPI/VU history and photographs. Very comprehensive – one of the best Warhol books.

Forced Entries: The Downtown Diaries: 1971-1973
Author: Carroll, Jim
(1987; Penguin Books)

The Year of the Barricades: A Journey Through 1968
Author: Caute, David

(1988; Harper & Row, New York)
Of note: Cultural, social and political history of 1968, including an account of the Warhol shooting. Quotes Gregory Corso: "You and your faggots and rich women and Velvet Undergrounds... I don't understand."

Lou Reed
Author: Cervera, Rafael
(288pp, 1990; Catedra, Madrid Spain, ISBN 84-376-0941-0)
Of note: Reed history, plus good English/Spanish lyrics.

Christgau's Record Guide
Author: Christgau, Robert
(1981; Ticknor & Fields, New Haven CT)
Of note: A collection of Christgau's 'Village Voice' reviews from the 1970s; includes reviews of all the VU and solo records from **Loaded** to 1981.

Lou Reed & The Velvet Underground
Author: Clapton, Diana
(128pp, 1982; Proteus, New York, ISBN: h/b 0 86276 0569, p/b 0 86276 0550; London. Current: 1987, Omnibus, London, ISBN: 0-7119-1-67-7)

The Amphetamine Manifesto
Author: Cohen, Harvey
(164pp, 1972; Olympia Press, New York)
Of note: Angus MacLise art plus quotes from his wife Hettie.

On Feet of Gold
Author: Cohen, Ira
(142pp, 1986; Synergetic, Oracle AZ, ISBN: 0-907791-107; Synergetic, London)
Of note: Includes a poem by Angus MacLise.

Cold-Drill 1991
Author: Cohen, Ira, edited by Bob Moore
(194pp, 1991; Department of English, Boise State U., Boise Idaho, ISBN: 0890-0086)
Of note: Ira Cohen writings plus a CD of his readings.

Andy Warhol
Author: Crone, Rainer
(332pp, 1970; Praeger, New York, ISBN: 76-129866)
Of note: Includes two photographs of Nico and a history of the Factory/EPI.

Lou Reed
Author: Destefanni, Fabio and Fabio Rametta
(131pp, 1981; Gammalibri, Milan Italy)
Of note: Biography, album by album summary and discography in Italian.

Growing Up In Public
Author: Doggett, Peter
(200pp, 1991; Omnibus, London, ISBN: 07119-24848)
Of note: Biography of Lou Reed, including photographs

The Films Of Andy Warhol:
    A Seven Week Introduction
Author: Easterwood, Kurt and E. S. Thiese
(52pp, 1990; San Francisco Cinematheque, San Francisco CA)
Of note: Essays on Warhol's films.

Age of Rock 2
Author: Eisen, Jonathan (ed.)
(1970; Vintage, New York)
Of note: Includes an interview with Danny Fields, in which he recalls Nico's first visit to the Factory and her affair with Jim Morrison.

La Dolce Vita
Author: Fellini, Federico
(276pp, 1961; Ballentine, New York)
Of note: Illustrated film script including some photographs of Nico.

Andy Warhol: The Factory Years 1964-1967
Author: Finkelstein, Nat
(96pp, 1989; St. Martin's Press, New York, ISBN: 0-312-02857-1; Sidgewick & Jackson, London, ISBN: 0-283-99871-7)
Of note: 1. Includes great VU/EPI photographs.
2. Also published in Holland as **Andy Warhol: 'Oh this is fabulous,' The Silver Age at the Factory**. Bebert Editions, Rotterdam, 1989, ISBN: 90-90370-95-6.

Andy Warhol: Films and Paintings
Author: Gidal, Peter
(1971; E. P. Dutton, New York; Studio Vista, London)

Materialist Film
Author: Gidal, Peter
(1989; Routledge and Kegan Paul, London, ISBN: 0-415-00382-2)

Photographs
Author: Ginsberg, Allen
(1990; Twelve Tree Press, Altadena CA)
Of note: Includes full-page portrait of Lou Reed from September 1984.

The Jefferson Airplane and the San Francisco Sound
Author: Gleason, Ralph J.
(June 1969; Ballantine Books, New York)
Of note: Interesting for its scathing review of a 1966 EPI Fillmore performance: "Nico, the whip girl, looks like Mick Jagger in drag... Bad condensation of all the bum

trips of the Trips Festival... The Velvet Underpants sang a song about whips. It was all very campy and very Greenwich Village sick... The Velvet Underground was really pretty lame."

Goldstein's Greatest Hits
Author: Goldstein, Richard
(1970; Prentice-Hall, New York)
Of note: Includes a reprint of Goldstein's 1966 'New York' magazine article, "A Quiet Evening at the Balloon Farm," which details the VU/EPI at the Dom.

The New Bohemia
Author: Gruen, John
(184pp, 1966; Grosset & Dunlap, New York, ISBN: 1-55652-097-2. Current: 1991, A Capella Books, US, ISBN: 1-55652-097-2)
Of note: Includes brief coverage of the EPI and stills from "The Chelsea Girls" and "Lupe" (with Edie Sedgwick).

The Art of Rock: Posters From Presley to Punk
Author: Grushkin, Paul D.
(516pp, 1987; Abbeville Press, New York, ISBN: 0-89659-584-6. Current: 1991, Artabras, US, ISBN: 0-89660-025-4)
Of note: Reproduces five vintage VU posters.

Loner at the Ball: Life of Andy Warhol
Author: Guiles, Fred Lawrence
(420pp, 1989; Bantam Press, London, ISBN: 0-593-01540-1; p/b 1990, Black Swan, London, ISBN: 0-552-99407-3)
Of note: VU/EPI/Nico history.

The Andy Warhol Diaries
Author: Hackett, Pat (ed.)
(807pp, May 1989; Warner Books, New York, ISBN: 0-446-51426-8; Simon & Schuster, London, ISBN: 0-671-69697-1. Current: 1992, Pan Books, London, ISBN: 0-330-31524-2, p/b)
Of note: Paperback edition includes index.

Gay Rock
Author: Haro Ibars, Eduardo
(223pp, 1975; Jucar, Madrid Spain, ISBN: 84-334-0231-5)
Of note: 1. Includes a chapter on Lou Reed and the VU.
2. Two poems attributed to Reed ("Love Song of the City" and "I Have Known Strange Hawks and Etiquettes") are not his work.
3. Text in Spanish.

Abdication of the Throne of Hell
Author: Heliczer, Piero
(48pp, 1981; Amsterdam School of Poetry, Amsterdam Holland, ISBN: 90-6512-010-6)
Of note: Collection of poems.

The Perfect Detective
Author: Heliczer, Piero
(40pp, 1989; Sovo Productions, Amsterdam Holland, ISBN: 90-72789-02-4)
Of note: Poems and other writings.

The Soap Opera
Author: Heliczer, Piero
(36pp, Trigham Press, London)
Of note: Limited edition of 500.

Rock 'N' Roll Babylon
Author: Herman, Gary
(192pp, 1982; Pedigree, New York and Toronto Canada, ISBN: 0-399-50641-1; 1989, Plexus, London, ISBN: 0-85965-131-2)

Allegories of Cinema: American Film in the Sixties
Author: James, David E.
(1989; Princeton University Press, Princeton NJ)

Feed-Back – The Legend of The Velvet Underground
Author: Julia, Ignacio
(98pp, 1986; Ruta 66, Barcelona Spain)
Of note: Large-format, well-illustrated book of the VU story, based around 1985 interviews with Sterling. Companion English translation with different graphics published by the Velvet Underground Appreciation Society in 1988.

Rock One Hundred
Author: Kaye, Lenny and David Dalton
(1977; Grosset and Dunlap, New York)
Of note: Great rock history; devotes a chapter to the VU, and reprints the poster advertising the VU at Poor Richard's, Chicago, summer 1966 (which first appeared in Aspen Magazine #3).

Stargazer: Andy Warhol's World and His Films
Author: Koch, Stephen
(156pp, 1973 & 1985; Marion Boyars Publishers, New York & London, ISBN: 0-7145-1037. Current: 1991, Marion Boyars, London, ISBN: 0-7145-2920-6)
Of note: 1. Includes VU/Factory photographs.
2. French edition: Chene, 1973, as **Hyperstar**.
3. 1985 second edition has new introduction by Koch.

Pre-Pop Warhol
Author: Kornbluth, Jesse
(1988; Random House, New York)

The Theatre of Mixed Means
Author: Kostelanetz, Richard
(1968; Dial)

Andy Warhol Et Al: The FBI File on Andy Warhol
Author: Kramer, Margia
(1988; UnSub Press, New York)

133

Flashing On The 60s
Author: Law, Lisa
(143pp, 1987; Chronicle Books, San Francisco CA, ISBN: 0-87701-465-5)

The Velvet Underground
Author: Leigh, Michael
(192pp, 1963; McFadden, New York)
Of note: The trashy paperback that provided the band's name. Reprinted in England in 1991 by Creation Press.

The Velvet Underground Revisited
Author: Leigh, Michael
(McFadden, New York)

Pop Art
Author: Lippard, Lucy R. (ed.)
(216pp, 1966; Praeger Publishers, New York; Thames & Hudson (World of Art Series), London, ISBN: 0-500-20052-1)
Of note: Warhol's life is well-documented here.

Nico
Author: Lundbye, Vagn
(1969; Berg, Ringkobing Denmark)
Of note: *Very* strange and uniquely wonderful Danish novel, using Nico as its inspirational focus. Some pages are blank, others repeat a single photograph of Nico; some repeat a short phrase, others just say 'Nico' over and over. Published with pages uncut top and bottom. Text in Danish.

The Cloud Doctrine
Author: MacLise, Angus
(Dreamweapon Press, Kathmandu, Nepal)

The Map of Dusk
Author: MacLise, Angus
(50pp, 1984; SZ Press, New York, ISBN: 0-930125-02-9)
Of note: Poetry, drawings, photograph of Angus.

Checklist: Angus MacLise Collection
Author: Malanga, Gerard (compiler)
(51pp, 1981; Dia Foundation, New York)
Of note: Extensive compilation of Angus' work.

Little Ceasar #9
Author: Malanga, Gerard (ed.)
(420pp, 1979; Dennis Cooper/Little Caesar Press, Los Angeles CA)
Of note: With a long letter from Sterling Morrison, plus work by Piero Heliczer, Angus MacLise, LaMonte Young, Gerard Malanga.

Canciones
Author: Manzano, Alberto (ed.)
(196pp, 1990; Espiral, Madrid Spain, ISBN: 84-245-0549-2)
Of note: Includes Lou Reed solo lyrics in English and Spanish.

Lou Reed – Canciones
Author: Manzano, Alberto (translator)
(143pp, 1988; Editorial Fundamentos, Madrid Spain, ISBN: 84-245-0502-6)
Of note: Very accurate English/ Spanish edition of VU lyrics.

Picado
Author: Manzano, Alberto (ed.)
(240pp, 1979; Zafo/Pastanaga, Barcelona Spain, ISBN: 84-85348-02-8)
Of note: Uninformed VU history, with English/Spanish lyrics.

Poetas Malditos del Rock
Author: Manzano, Alberto (ed.)
(176pp, 1986; Espiral, Madrid Spain, ISBN: 84-245-0465-8)
Of note: Includes selected John Cale lyrics from 1973-1985, in English and Spanish.

Reinas del Rock
Author: Manzano, Alberto (ed.)
(174pp, 1987; Espiral, Madrid Spain, ISBN: 245-0500-X)
Of note: Lyrics by Patti Smith, Laurie Anderson, Kate Bush and Nico, in English and Spanish.

Rock and Other Four Letter Words
Author: Marks, J & Linda Eastman
(1968; Bantam, New York)
Of note: 1. Photographic history of rock, including a full-page photograph of the EPI on stage.
2. The album of the same name contains no VU references.

The Medium Is The Massage
Author: McLuhan, Marshall
(160pp, March 1967; Random House, New York)
Of note: Includes two-page photographic section on the VU/EPI.

Andy Warhol: A Retrospective
Author: McShine, Kynaston (ed.)
(1989; The Museum of Modern Art, New York, ISBN: 0-87070-681-0)

Movie Journal: The Rise of a New American Cinema, 1959-1971
Author: Mekas, Jonas
(434pp, 1972; MacMillian, New York)
Of note: Includes reviews of the VU at the Dom and 'The Chelsea Girls'.

The Aesthtics of Rock
Author: Meltzer, Richard
(1970; Something Else, New York. Current: 1987, Da Capo Press, London, ISBN: 0-306-80287-2)
Of note: Gonzo-style rock history, with many VU/Nico references.

Words & Music – Lou Reed
Author: Miles, Barry (ed.)
(32pp, 1980; Wise Publications, London, ISBN: 0-86001-591-2)
Of note: History of Lou Reed's solo career, recounted in quotes dressed up as newspaper clippings, plus unreliable lyrics.

Popsmuk
Author: Oets, Pim, and Gijsbert Hanekroot
(144pp, 1972; Born, Amsterdam Holland)
Of note: Includes 14 pages on the VU, with interviews and full-page photographs of Nico, Moe, John and Lou.

Rock Dreams
Author: Peellaert, Guy, and Nik Cohn
(174pp, Popular Library, N Y, ISBN: 445-08313-795)
Of note: Highly stylised paintings of rock legends, including paintings of the VU and of Lou Reed.

Yardbirds
Author: Platt, John, Chris Dreja and Jim McCarty
(1983; Sidgwick & Jackson, London)
Of note: This history of the Yardbids includes Dreja's comments on Andy, Lou and the VU's 1966 "Mod wedding" performance. Also confirms that the Yardbirds performed **I'm Waiting For The Man** live.

Beyond Thought and Expression
Author: Reed, Lou
(192pp, 1991, Hyperion, New York, ISBN 1-562-993-9; 176pp, 1992, Viking, London, ISBN 0-670-845-329)
Of note: Selected lyrics, with occasional annotations by Reed, and including Reed's interviews with Vaclav Havel and Hubert Selby Jr.

New York
Author: Reed, Lou
(80pp, 1989; Warner Brothers Publishing, Secacus NJ)
Of note: 1. Songbook of lyrics and music from the album. 2. Includes photographs of Lou.

Songs For Drella
Author: Reed, Lou and John Cale
(92pp, 1990; Warner Brothers Publications, New York)
Of note: Songbook of words and music.

Transformer
Author: Reed, Lou
(1973; Charles Hansen, New York)
Of note: Lyrics and music songbook of the album.

The World
Author: Reed, Lou, edited by Ann Waldman
(1975; New York)
Of note: Poems by Lou Reed.

An Introduction to the American Underground Film
Author: Renan, Sheldon
(318pp, 1967; E. P. Dutton, New York, ISBN: 289-37061-2)
Of note: UK edition published in 1968 by Studio Vista, London.

The Rock Scene
Author: Robinson, Richard and Andy Zwerling
(April 1971; Pyramid Books, New York)
Of note: Excellent rock paperback which includes Velvet Underground and Lou Reed material. Back cover text asks, "Who is the finest band in the land? Led Zeppelin, The Velvet Underground, The Dead, The Stooges?"

The Rock Revolution
Author: Robinson, Richard (ed.)
(1973; Curtiss Books, New York)
Of note: 1. Good collection of rock writing: includes VU references in Lenny Kaye's "East Coast Rock" and Lester Bangs' "The Heavy Metal Kids" and "Glitter Rock."
2. Extensive year-by-year discography includes VU and solo LPs.

In Dreams Begin Responsibilities
Author: Schwartz, Delmore
(202pp, 1938; New Directions, New York)
Of note: Reprinted in 1978 by New Direction Books, London, ISBN: 0-8112-0680-7.

One-Trick Pony
Author: Simon, Paul
(95pp, 1980; Knopf, New York, ISBN: h/b 0-394-51381-9, p/b 0-394-73961-2)
Of note: Film script with photographs; Lou Reed had a part in the film as a 'hit producer.'

Visionary Film: The American Avant-Garde 1943-1978
Author: Sitney, P. Adams
(1979; Oxford University Press, New York, ISBN: 0-19-502486-9)

Warhol: Conversations About the Artist
Author: Smith, Patrick S.
(1988; UMI Research Press, Ann Arbor MI)

Andy Warhol's Art and Films
Author: Smith, Patrick S.
(1986; UMI Research Press, Ann Arbor MI)

Aquarian Odyssey: A Photographic Trip Into The 60s
Author: Snyder, Don
(1979; Liveright, New York, ISBN: 0-87140-639-X)
Of note: Includes photographs of Angus MacLise plus a Malanga poem.

The S.C.U.M. Manifesto
Author: Solanas, Valerie
(52pp, 1968; Olympia Press, New York. Current: 1988, Phoenix, London, ISBN: 0-948984-03-1)
Of note: It was Valerie Solanis who shot and seriously wounded Andy Warhol in 1968.

No One Waved Goodbye
Author: Somma, Robert (ed.)
(1971; 121pp, Outerbridge & Dienstfrui, New York)
Of note: Includes an essay by Lou Reed and an interview with Danny Fields about Nico and Brian Jones.

Edie: An American Biography
Author: Stein, Jean and George Plimpton
(456pp, 1982; Knopf, New York, ISBN: 394-48819-9. Current: 1992, Pimlico, London, ISBN: 0-7126-5252-3)

Beyond The Velvet Underground
Author: Thompson, Dave
(96pp, 1989; Omnibus, New York & London, ISBN: 0-7119-1691-8)

Of note: Very loose history of the VU told through out-of-context quotes.

Lou Reed & The Velvets
Author: Trevena, Nigel
(1973; Bantam, London)
Of note: Early history.

Underground Film: A Critical History
Author: Tyler, Parker
(1969; Grove Press, New York)

John Cale
Author: Unknown (ed.)
(1990; 109pp, Germany)
Of note: 1. Cale biography with accurate lyrics in English and German, plus discography.
2. Limited edition of 500.

Lou Reed & The Velvet Underground
Author: Unknown (ed.)
(1985; 118pp, Germany)
Of note: Reed/VU lyrics in English and German, plus VU discography and recording info.

Nico
Author: Unknown (ed.)
(1990; 109pp, Germany)
Of note: Privately-printed collection of reviews, interviews, lyrics, photographs and discography.

All The Pretty People
Author: Various
(Stimula)
Of note: Unauthorized edition limited to 326 copies featuring poems by Reed: "The Man", "Dirt", "Street Hasseling", "The Slide".

The Best of Creem
Author: Various
(90pp, Creem Magazine, Detroit Michigan)
Of note: Includes Lester Bangs' article "Dead Lie the Velvets, Underground."

Lou Reed & The Velvet Underground
Author: Various
(8pp, Popster, Barcelona Spain)
Of note: Booklet of VU/Reed history with poster of Lou.

Lou Reed & The Velvet Underground
Author: Various
(64pp, 1976; Rock Comix, Barcelona Spain)

Rock'N'Roll Animal
Author: Various
(1979; Babylon)

SMS (Shit Must Stop)
Author: Various
(68pp, February 1968; Aspen/William Copley, New York)
Of note: Features a folder of drawings and poetry, "The Inner Pages", by Angus MacLise.

Stranded
Author: Various
Of note: A collection of essays about people's choices of 'Desert Island Discs'. Ellen Willis' Desert Island LP: the VU 'Golden Archive' collection.

Velvet Underground: Rock Manual #12
Author: Various
(208pp, 1990; Arcana Editrice, Milan Italy, ISBN: 88-85859-98-4)

Of note: 1. Good collection of various VU articles, interviews and discographies from 1966-1990.
2. Text in Italian.

Famous For Fifteen Minutes – My Years With Andy Warhol
Author: Violet, Ultra
(274pp, 1988; Harcourt Brace Jovanovich, Orlando FL, ISBN 0-15-130201-4; Metheun, London, ISBN 0-413-61530-8. Current: 1990, Mandarin, London, ISBN: 0-7493-0250-X, p/b)

Superstar
Author: Viva
(295pp, 1970; Putnam, New York, ISBN: 90-6008-056-4)
Of note: 1. VU/Factory tales.
2. Dutch edition published by Nieuwe Wieken in 1971.

Het Zoete Leven ("La Dolce Vita")
Author: Wallagh, Bob
(142pp, Mimosa Reeks, Amsterdam Holland)
Of note: 1. Novelized version of the screenplay.
2. Includes a still of Nico from the film.

New York 1940-1965
Author: Wallock, Leonard (ed.)
(1988; Rizzoli International Publications, New York)
Of note: 1. Excellent history of NYC arts scene.
2. Includes references to the VU and reproduces the cover of the first LP.

A
Author: Warhol, Andy
(451pp, 1968; Grove Press, New York)
Of note: A transcription of 24 hours of Factory life, with the ususal cast of characters. (Warhol paid two high school students, and Moe Tucker, to transcribe his tapes.

Moe did a great, fast job, but refused to include the dirty words, leaving spaces for Andy to go back and insert them.)

Andy Warhol
Author: Warhol, Andy
(474pp, February 1968; Worldwide Books, Stockholm Sweden)
Of note: 1. Lush book of photographs published for the Warhol exhibition at the Moderna Museum in Stockholm, 1968.
2. *The* book for Factory photos – the biggest selection ever published in one place. Includes photographs by Billy Name and Stephen Shore.

Andy Warhol, Cinema
Author: Warhol, Andy
(270pp, 1990; Les Editions Carre and Center Geo. Pompidou, Paris)
Of note: 1. Lavish retrospective, including many Factory shots, stills of Nico etc, with filmography.
2. Text in French.

Andy Warhol's Exposures
Author: Warhol, Andy
(260pp, 1979; Grosset & Dunlap, New York, ISBN: h/b 0-448-12850-0, p/b 0-448-12658-3)
Of note: Snapshots of the rich and famous and not so rich and famous. Quote from Elton John: "I got into rock and roll with the Velvet Underground in the sixties."

Andy Warhol's Index (Book)
Author: Warhol, Andy
(70pp, 1967; Random House, New York)
Of note: Contains many photographs of VU members, plus a cardboard record (with Lou's face printed on the disc) of Lou's and Nico's reactions on looking through a rough draft of the "Index" at a party.

The Philosophy of Andy Warhol (From A to B and Back Again)
Author: Warhol, Andy
(242pp, 1975; Harcourt Brace Jovanovich, New York, ISBN: 0-15-189050-1)

POPism: The Warhol '60s
Author: Warhol, Andy and Pat Hackett
(310pp, 1980; Harper & Row, New York, ISBN: 0-06-091062-3)
Of note: 1. Includes an account of the VU.
2. Warhol writes that **All Tomorrow's Parties** was his favorite VU song.

The Prints of Andy Warhol
Author: Warhol, Andy
(127pp, 1990; Museum of Modern Art/Cartier Foundation)

Warhol: A Postcard Book
Author: Warhol, Andy
(1989; Running Press Book Publishing, Philadelphia PA, ISBN: 0-89471-693-X)
Of note: Thirty postcards, including "Banana."

The Velvet Underground & Lou Reed
Author: West, Mike
(62pp, 1982; Babylon Books, Manchester UK, ISBN: 0 907188 13 3)
Of note: Collection of material drawn from "Different Times," a UK VU/Reed fanzine.

The Autobiography And Sex Life of Andy Warhol
Author: Wilcock, John
(124pp, 1971; Other Scenes, New York)
Of note: Interviews about Andy with his associates, including Lou Reed and Nico.

The Kandy-Kolored Tangerine-Flake Streamline Baby
Author: Wolfe, Tom
(1965; Farrar, Straus, & Giroux Inc, New York. Current: 1981, Pan/Picador, London, ISBN: 0-330-26525-3)

The Electric Kool-Aid Acid Test
Author: Wolfe, Tom
(1968; Farrar, Straus, & Giroux Inc, New York. Current: 1989; Black Swan, London, ISBN: 0-552-99366-2)

Andy Warhol In His Own Words
Author: Wrenn, Mike (ed.)
(94pp, 1991; Omnibus Press, London, ISBN: 0-7119-2400-7)
Of note: Includes several comments from Warhol on the VU/EPI, as well as photographs.

An Anthology – LaMonte Young
Author: Young, LaMonte
(68pp, 1963; Dia Foundation, New York)

Expanded Cinema
Author: Youngblood, Gene
(432pp, 1970; E. P. Dutton, Toronto Canada, ISBN: 0-525-47263-0)
Of note: Includes a review of and still from the film "Andy Warhol's Exploding Plastic Inevitable".

Velvet Underground-Related Magazine Articles

Author: Abrams, Bobby
Article: Review of **Live at Max's**
Magazine: Phonograph Record
(August 1972, Los Angeles CA)
Of note: Long review: "It will survive to tell of our age, of our time, to denote an epic moment in the development of an American aesthetic."

Author: Bangs, Lester
Article: Review of the third LP
Magazine: Rolling Stone
(No. 33, 17 May 1968, San Francisco CA)
Of note: Lester Bangs' first review for Rolling Stone.

Author: Bangs, Lester
Article: "Dead Lie The Velvets, Underground"
Magazine: Creem
(Vol. 3, No. 2, May 1971, Detroit MI)
Of note: The definitive VU article by Lester Bangs. Reprinted in **The Best of Creem**, 1981. For reasons known only to Greil Marcus, this is not included in the Bangs collection **Psychotic Reactions and Carburetor**

Dung. Classic eulogy/overview: "As Lou said recently, 'I think a lot of our music is about growing up, in a way. It's nice to be mature, to be able to meet things rationally sometimes instead of with all this nervous sort of emotionalism.'"

Author: Blauner, Peter
Article: "Rock Noir"
Magazine: New York
(27 November 1989, New York)
Of note: Interviews with Cale and Reed about the pair's **Songs for Drella** project in memory of Andy Warhol.

Author: Brown, Allan
Article: "White Heat"
Magazine: Melody Maker
(30 June 1990, London)
Of note: Review of the Cartier reunion.

Author: Carroll, Cath
Article: Review of **Another View**
Magazine: New Musical Express
(21 February 1987, London)
Of note: "...goes to prove that the gang can be as self-indulgent as anyone else."

Author: Carroll, Paul
Article: "What's A Warhol?"
Magazine: Playboy
(September 1969, Chicago IL)
Of note: Two pages of Warhol Xerox self-portraits, along with Factory, Nico and EPI stories.

Author: Cervera, Rafa
Article: "Hijos de V.U."
Magazine: Ruta 66
(June 1986, Barcelona Spain)
Of note: Assesses the VU's musical legacy. Text in Spanish.

Author: Cromelin, Richard
Article: "Lou Reed & The Velvet Underground"
Magazine: Phonograph Record
(October 1973, Los Angeles CA)
Of note: 1. Retrospective: "It was pretend, it was fantasy, but the magic and the mystery was the complete union of their lives with the fantasy."
2. Issue also features a review of Lou Reed's **Berlin** by David Johansen, then singer with the New York Dolls: "I think this album's a hoot. I hope he gets away with it."

Author: Crucifix, Jean-Luc
Article: "L'Ombre Du Velvet"
Magazine: Rock-Folk
(No. 59, December 1971, Paris)
Of note: 1. History: "...groupe quasi-mythique qui evolue solitaire au sein des Ameriques decadentes, dans l'orgie et la perversite new-yorkaises."
2. Good photographs of the Moe-Willie line-up.
3. Text in French.

Author: Doggett, Peter
Article: "Lou Reed – High School Pop and Garage Rock"
Magazine: Record Collector
(No. 154, June 1992, London)
Of note: 1. A detailed and highly informative piece on Lou's pre-VU years, written by Reed's biographer.
2. This issue of the magazine also includes a knowledgable and considered piece by Doggett on the 3-CD Reed retrospective **Between Thought and Expression**.

Author: Edmonds, Ben
Article: "The Velvet Underground"
Magazine: Fusion
(No. 49, 5 February 1971, Boston MA)
Of note: A long review of **Loaded**: "They travel in circles seldom glimpsed by even the heaviest of rock and roll bands."

Author: Eliscu, Lisa
Article: "A Rock Band Can Be a Form of Yoga"
Magazine: Crawdaddy
(Vol. 4, No. 4, January 1970, New York)
Of note: Odd overview of the 1970 VU: "I threw the I Ching and got a strange set of hexagrams..."

Author: Fevret, Christian
Article: "Nothing Compares to VU"
Magazine: New Musical Express
(27 June 1990, London)
Of note: Story, with photographs, of the Cartier reunion – "...a thousand journalists were stiff with excitement..."

Author: Fevret, Christian
Article: "Helden"
Magazine: Spex
(No. 9, September 1990, Cologne Germany)
Of note: Cover story and interviews with the band members in Paris 1990, with several rare photographs. Text in German.

Author: Fevret, Christian and David Swift
Article: "The Exploding Plastic Interview (part 1)"
Magazine: New Musical Express
(6 October 1990, London)
Of note: Compilation of 1990 Paris interviews with all four members, plus many early photographs. Essential update/retro.

Author: Fevret, Christian and David Swift
Article: "The Exploding Plastic Interview (part 2)"
Magazine: New Musical Express
(13 October 1990, London)
Of note: Continuation of above.

Author: Fricke, David and Allan Jones
Article: "A Farewell to Andy"
Magazine: Melody Maker
(28 April 1990, London)
Of note: Cover story chat with Lou, giving a good perspective on **Songs for Drella** and the VU.

Author: Fuchs-Gambock, Michael, Norbert Sorg
Article: "Die Blumen Des Bosen"
Magazine: Zounds
(No. 2, February 1992, Stuttgart Germany)
Of note: Cover story on Lou, plus feature article on 25th anniversary of the **VU & Nico** LP with several rare photographs.

Author: Gangewere, R. Jay
Article: "Talking to Mark Francis"
Magazine: Carnegie Magazine
(Vol. LX, No. 4, July/August 1990, Pittsburgh PA)
Of note: Interview with the man who is setting up The Andy Warhol Museum, which will include a VU section.

Author: Glover, Tony
Magazine: Rolling Stone
(3 August 1972, San Francisco CA)
Of note: Review of **Live at Max's**.

Author: Goldberg, Danny
Article: "Beyond Warhol, The Velvet Underground, Loaded"
Magazine: Circus
(February 1971, New York)
Of note: "The Velvets' old professor, Delmore Schwartz, once wrote, 'a cup of coffee can destroy your sadness', and the Velvet Underground were New York's cup of coffee throughout 1970's summer smog."

Author: Greenfield, Robert
Article: "C/o The Velvet Underground, New York, NY"
Magazine: Fusion
(No. 8, 6 March 1970, Boston MA)
Of note: Good VU history, and one of the few VU-era interviews with Sterling ("Sterling Morrison was once described as the most under-rated person living."). Plus a collection of Warhol quotes.

Author: Hogg, Brian
Article: "Velvet Underground"
Magazine: Bam Balam
(No. 14, September 1982, Dunbar, East Lothian, Scotland)
Of note: Fanzine with 8-page VU history.

Author: Hogg, Brian
Article: "Velvet Underground: Discography"
Magazine: Record Collector
(No. 49, September 1983, London)
Of note: Gives values of records for collectors.

Author: Jones, Allan
Article: Review of V.U.
Magazine: Melody Maker
(16 February 1985, London)
Of note: "Twenty years on, listening to the Velvet Underground is still like dancing with lightning....They remain, arguably, the most influential group in the history of rock..."

Author: Jones, Nick
Article: "New Wave USA"
Magazine: Melody Maker
(25 November 1967, London)
Of note: Article on new US bands, with a brief VU mention plus photograph.

Author: Julia, Ignacio
Article: "En Pecuerdo De Aquel Famoso Platano"
Magazine: Prima Linea
(August 1990, Barcelona Spain)
Of note: Glossy insider's account of the 1990 Cartier show (riding in the limo with Sterling, etc.), with color photographs.

Author: Julia, Ignacio
Article: "Perseguido Por El Pasado"
Magazine: Ruta 66
(December 1988, Barcelona Spain)
Of note: Cale interview discussing the origins of **Songs for Drella**, Nico's death and VU days, plus Cale discography. Text in Spanish.

Author: Julia, Ignacio
Article: "Requiem Por Un Bote De Sopa Campbell"
Magazine: Ruta 66
(No. 48, February 1990, Barcelona Spain)
Of note: Six-page cover story about Ignacio's visit to New York for the **Drella** concerts in December 1989. Includes interviews with Cale, Reed, Malanga, and a Warhol chronology. Text in Spanish.

Author: Julia, Ignacio
Article: "Maureen Tucker: Pasiones Domesticas"
Magazine: Ruta 66
(October 1987, Barcelona Spain)
Of note: Interview with Moe about VU days.

Author: Julia, Ignacio, M.C. Kostek, Philip Milstein
Article: "New York 1968/Paris 1990"
Magazine: Ruta 66
(No. 54, September 1990, Barcelona Spain)
Of note: Eight-page section of the magazine that also served as program for the 10-day VU/Warhol exhibition in Barcelona, 19-29 September 1990. Many rare photographs and posters from both the 60s and the 1990 Cartier reunion. Text in Spanish.

Author: Kaye, Lenny
Article: **Loaded** review
Magazine: Rolling Stone
(24 December 1970, San Francisco CA)
Of note: Good tribute/history/review... "Easily one of the best albums to show up this or any other year".

Author: Kemp, Mark
Article: "15 Minutes with You"
Magazine: Option
(No. 33, July/August 1990, Los Angeles CA)
Of note: Long interviews with John and Lou about **Songs for Drella**, and the VU's roots.

Author: Kent, Nick
Article: "Friendly Patchwork of Ageing Velvet"
Magazine: The Sunday Correspondent
(24 June 1990, London)
Of note: A good story on the 1990 reunion ("...a unique musical chemistry that still smoulders after 22 dank, mostly bitter years apart.")

Author: Kirsch, Michele
Article: "Nico: Last of the Bohemians"
Magazine: New Musical Express
(30 July 1988, London)
Of note: Obituary.

Author: Lake, Steve
Article: "Rock Giants: Velvet Underground – Opening the Doors of Perception"
Magazine: Melody Maker
(25 May 1974, London)
Of note: VU history.

Author: Lycett, Andrew
Article: "Velvet Underground: They're Just Plain Folks"
Magazine: Melody Maker
(17 April 1971, London)
Of note: History of the group.

Author: Marsh, Dave
Article: "Desertshore"
Magazine: Creem
(December 1970, Detroit MI)
Of note: A review of Nico's album **Desertshore**.

Author: McCombs, Larry
Article: "Chicago Happenings"
Magazine: Boston Broadside
(July 1966, Boston MA)
Of note: 1. Review of the EPI at Poor Richard's: "the music is lost in the chaos of noise. Are there children chanting or singing?... Then it goes on and on and on and on... you wish it would stop."
2. Reprinted in Zig Zag No. 41.

Author: McGuire, Wayne
Article: "The Boston Sound/The Velvet Underground & Mel Lyman"
Magazine: Crawdaddy
(No. 17, August 1968, New York)
Of note: Far-ranging five-page essay on the VU's virtues: "Put quite simply, the Velvet Underground is the most vital and significant group in the world today. They are at the firey center of the twentieth century dilemma, as was Nietzsche."

Author: Meredith, Noel
Article: Review of VU concert at St. Alban's City Hall
Magazine: Melody Maker
(2 December 1972, London)

Author: Nordlie, Tom and Michael Brennan
Article: "Beginning to See the Light"
Magazine: Applause/Florida Alligator
(6 December 1985, Gainesville FL)
Of note: Fine overview of the band's history, with good new (1985) quotes from Moe: "I would have liked to have had the opportunity to do even one more album with John. We were all much more attuned to each other after two years than on the first album."

Author: Nusser, Richard
Article: "No Pale Imitation"
Magazine: Village Voice
(2 July 1970, New York)
Of note: Intelligent review of a VU gig at Max's Kansas City.

Author: Pantsios, Anastasia
Article: "Velvet Underground Surfaces in Cleveland"
Magazine: The Scene
(6-12 May 1971, Cleveland OH)
Of note: Live review of post-Lou VU: "...it is a little difficult to see what part Reed must have played in the group, becaue they don't seem to be missing a piece anywhere."

Author: Pearlman, Sandy
Article: "Velvet Underground"
Magazine: Crawdaddy
(No. 16, June 1968, New York)
Of note: Favorable but wobbly review of **White Light**: "...the Velvet's repetition scene makes it hard to tell

whether they're playing badly or not (hypnosis plus practice makes perfect), which was an always pressing problem for the Banana album."

Author: Pouncey, Edwin
Article: "Going Underground"
Magazine: New Musical Express
(2 December 1989, London)
Of note: Feature review of the first LP – "...songs that still shimmer with an unearthly light..." – giving the album a rating of 9.

Author: Rauvolf, Joseph
Article: "Good Bye Andy"
Magazine: Reflex
(11 July 1990, Prague, Czechoslovakia)
Of note: Six pages of color photographs plus story of the 1990 reunion. Text in Czech.

Unmuzzled Ox
Author: Reed, Lou, edited by Michael Andre
(160pp, 1976; Michael Andre, N Y, ISSN: 0049-5557)
Of note: Poems by Lou Reed.

Author: Richman, Jonathan
Article: The Velvet Underground and Nico
Magazine: Vibrations
(July 1967, Boston MA)
Of note: Review of the first LP, with photographs of a VU performance in Boston and of Warhol with Nico on Boston Common.

Author: Snow, Mat
Article: "Yes, We Have No Bananas"
Magazine: New Musical Express
(3 May 1986, London)
Of note: Review of UK box set: "...most of all, it's the

sense of REAL people saying real things in a strikingly new and pertinent way that endures most. Some, if not all, of human life is here."

Author: Snow, Mat
Article: "The Best of The Velvet Underground"
Magazine: Q
(December 1989, London)
Of note: Review, giving the record 4 stars.

Author: Solanas, Jane
Article: "Oh God, Not The Bloody Velvets Again"
Magazine: New Musical Express
(26 April 1986, London)
Of note: Review of TV's "South Bank Show": "...the cult of the Velvets is perhaps the strongest belonging to any rock 'n' roll band ever... the cult remains powerful because the Velvets' music is unique, timeless..."

Author: Taylor, Paul
Article: "The Golden Underground"
Magazine: Village Voice
(10 July 1990, New York)
Of note: A look at Cartier's financial roots in South Africa.

Author: Trakin, Roy
Article: "I, Me, Mine"
Magazine: Musician
(March 1980, New York)
Of note: The ten best LPs of the 1970s: **Loaded** is #3: "...an amazing barometer for what eventually went down in the seventies." (#1 was **Exile on Main Street**, #2 **Ziggy Stardust**)

Author: Ungemuth, N., M. Zisman
Article: "Freres Ennemis"
Magazine: Guitare & Claviers
(No. 109, June 1990, Paris)
Of note: Interviews with Lou and John about **Songs for Drella**. Text in French.

Author: Video, E.I.
Article: Andy Warhol
Magazine: Record Mirror
(28 February 1987, London)
Of note: Obituary.

Author: Watts, Michael
Article: Review of **Loaded**
Magazine: Melody Maker
(13 March 1971, London)

Author: Weisberg, Jacob
Article: 'Washington Diarist' column: "Crushed Velvet"
Magazine: The New Republic
(5 March 1990, Washington DC)
Of note: Musings on Czechoslovakia's 'Velvet Revolution' – "...the revolution that made Czechoslovakia safe for the Velvet Underground."

Author: Welch, Chris
Article: Review of **Sweet Jane** 45
Magazine: Melody Maker
(11 May 1974, London)

Author: Wilkes, Jane
Article: "Another View"
Magazine: Record Mirror
(28 February 1987, London)
Of note: Album review: "...best left on the shelf from whence it came."

Author: Williams, Richard
Article: Review of **Squeeze** LP
Magazine: Melody Maker
(10 February 1973, London)

Author: Williams, Richard
Article: Review of the band live at the Speakeasy pub
Magazine: Melody Maker
(16 October 1971, London)
Of note: "...a travesty, a masquerade." (Plus VU tour ads in back pages.)

Author: Williams, Richard
Magazine: Melody Maker
(18 September 1971, London)
Of note: Reviews of the reissues of the first and third LPs.

Author: Williams, Richard
Article: Review of reissues of **White Light/White Heat** and **Chelsea Girl**
Magazine: Melody Maker
(23 October 1971, London)

Author: Willis, Ellen
Article: "And Then?"
Magazine: Village Voice
(3 July 1990, New York)
Of note: Short item on the Cartier reunion – "Yes, the 90s have definitely begun."

Author: Wilson, Tom
Magazine: Forced Exposure
Article: "Music Factory"
(No. 7/8, 1988, Boston MA)
Of note: Transcription of "Music Factory" interview with John and Lou.

Note: The following articles, listed alphabetically by magazine title, are by authors unknown.

Magazine: Art in America
Article: "A Catalog Raisonne of Warhol's Gestures"
(May/June 1971, New York)
Of note: Cover story about the first Warhol retrospective at the Whitney Museum. Includes color photograph of Nico from "**** (Four Stars)," and covers the E.P.I. and the 'Mod wedding'. Describes Nico as a "singer of cryptic dirges whose voice has been likened to wind in a drainpipe."

Magazine: Circus
Article: "Velvet Underground: Music and Mystique Unveiled"
(August 1970, New York)
Of note: Two-page article.

Magazine: Creem
Article: "'Some Kinda Love...' Twenty Years of The Velvet Underground"
(Vol. 19, No. 1, November 1987, Los Angeles CA)
Of note: Cover story. including interviews with Reed, Cale, Nico, Moe, Sterling, Doug and LaMonte Young.

Magazine: Entertainment Weekly
Article: "The 35 Greatest Acts of All Time"
(No. 39, 9 November 1990, New York)
Of note: VU placed at #9 (Places the VU above Springsteen, Prince, Sex Pistols, The Who, Bowie, Madonna, Otis Redding, Sly Stone, Beach Boys, Janis Joplin, Little Richard, Byrds, Kinks & Supremes; behind the Stones, Elvis, Dylan, Beatles, Jimi Hendrix, James Brown, Chuck Berry & Led Zeppelin).

Magazine: Evergreen Review
Article: "Dragtime and Drugtime"
(April 1967, New York)
Of note: Describes the evolution of Warhol's colors "into arbitrary psychedelic spectra, related to the fluent kaleidoscope of his Velvet Underground projector."

Magazine: Eye
(August 1968, New York)
Of note: Includes an article about Los Angeles' Castle, a wonderful, spooky place up in the Hollywood hills which was frequently rented to rock bands and was home to the VU in May 1966. LA critic Digby Diehl interviews Nico, who conducts a tour of the Castle.

Magazine: Eye
Article: "What Has Andy Warhol's Gang Been Up To?"
(October 1968, New York)
Of note: Includes two great two-page Factory group shots (one color, one b&w), including Nico. Extensive text with Nico references.

Magazine: The Fifth Estate
(Vol. 1, No. 18, Nov 15-30 1966, Detroit Michigan)
Of note: Article on the 'Mod Wedding' (see Timeline, 1966).

Magazine: Film Culture
(No. 45 – 'Superstar' issue, Summer 1968, New York)
Of note: Issue guest edited by Gerard Malanga. Includes articles on "Chelsea Girls" and many photobooth pictures of Nico.

Magazine: Fusion
Article: "A Very Pure and Old-Fashioned Christmas"
(22 January 1971, Boston MA)
Of note: 1. A two-page poem by Lou Reed.
2. **Loaded** is also featured in this issue as one of the 'Critics' Favourite' LPs of 1970.

Magazine: Fusion
Article: "We Are the People"
(5 March 1971, Boston MA)
Of note: A poem by Lou Reed.

Magazine: The History of Rock
(Vol. 5, No. 51, 1982, London)
Of note: Five-page article on the VU's history.

Magazine: Hullabaloo
Article: "The Above-Ground Sound of the Velvet Underground"
(Vol. 3, No. 4, May/June 1968, New York)
Of note: One-page blurb announcing imminent fame due to **White Light** release – "Welcome to the hot glare of fame, fortune and publicity, group!". Plus **White Light** full-page ad: "Come. Step softly into the inevitable world of THE VELVET UNDERGROUND..."and "Design a VU Subway Token Contest" ad.

Magazine: Jazz and Pop
Article: "The New Rock"
(June 1967, New York)
Of note: Negative review of the first Velvet Underground LP.

Magazine: Jazz and Pop
Article: Frank Zappa interview
(October 1967, New York)
Of note: Lengthy interview in which Zappa describes the VU as an example of "electric folk music."

Magazine: Life
Article: "What's Happening?"
(27 May 1966, New York)
Of note: Discotheque article includes two page color photograph of VU/EPI at 'The Trip' in Los Angeles.

Magazine: Life
Article: "Winners and Losers"
(10 January 1969 – "68 Special – The Incredible Year', New York)
Of note: Includes small photograph of Warhol: "He is back to art and making films of Viva, Nico and pals. May it always be like that."

Magazine: Melody Maker
Article: Review of **White Light/White Heat**
(6 July 1968, London)
Of note: Short review: "...utterly pretentious, unbelievably monotonous..."

Magazine: Melody Maker
Article: "The Velvet Underground"
(17 May 1969, London)
Of note: Review of the third LP.

Magazine: Melody Maker
Article: "Blind Date"
(2 January 1971, London)
Of note: Elton John review of the VU track **Rock & Roll** in the 'Blind Date' series.

Magazine: Melody Maker
Article: "History of the Velvets"
(18 September 1971, London)
Of note: Review of the UK reissues of the first and third LPs: "The first of these albums is one of the most important and influential rock records ever made. The second is the most organic and interesting extended work in rock."

Magazine: Melody Maker
Article: "Velvets Reform"
(29 January 1972, London)
Of note: Reed/Cale/Nico at the Bataclan Club, Paris – TV show/concert news item.

Magazine: Melody Maker
Article: Photograph and short report on the Bataclan show
(19 February 1972, London)
Of note: "The concert was attended by about a thousand people, with twice that number locked out and a minor 'speed-freak riot' in the foyer."

Magazine: Melody Maker
Article: "Max's Kansas City...Yawn"
(2 October 1972, London)
Of note: A visit to Max's Kansas City in 1972: "It's a pretty dull sort of place really you know."

Magazine: Melody Maker
Article: "Velvets Back on the Road with Eno"
(8 June 1974, London)
Of note: News story following a Kevin Ayres gig, 1 June, at which Eno, Nico, and John Cale played, suggesting that the latter three were planning to get together as a new line-up VU.

Magazine: Melody Maker
Article: "Sex in Rock"
(21 September 1974, London)
Of note: Mentions **The Murder Mystery**, **Venus In Furs**, **Sister Ray**, and **Some Kinda Love**.

Magazine: Melody Maker
Article: "Ahead of Their Time"
(2 December 1974, London)
Of note: Feature article.

Magazine: New Musical Express
Article: "Nico's Tribute To Andy"
(7 March 1987, London)
Of note: News story about Nico's forthcoming (12 March) concert at The Fridge, which is to be a tribute to Andy Warhol with Factory slides and Warhol videos.

Magazine: New Musical Express
Article: "Memorial Service for Nico"
(6 August 1988, London)
Of note: News item previewing memorial service to be held at St. John's Church, Holmefirth, near Huddersfield.

Magazine: New Musical Express
(3 September 1988, London)
Of note: News item about Moe and John supposedly playing on Lou's upcoming **New York** LP.

Magazine: Record Collector
Article: The Velvet Underground
(No. 120, August 1989, London)
Of note: Compact disc run-down.

Magazine: Record Mirror
Article: Review of **The Best of The Velvet Underground**
(2 December 1989, London)
Of note: "Arguably some of the greatest songs ever written and a yardstick for a generation of rock bands." 5 star rating.

Magazine: Rolling Stone
Article: "The GTOs"
(15 February 1969, San Francisco CA)
Of note: Article quotes Miss Christine: "Mercy and I sent the Velvet Underground a dozen roses with our pictures on the back. You can't be too subtle."

Magazine: Rolling Stone
Article: "Shards of Velvet Afloat in London"
(18 February 1971, San Francisco CA)
Of note: On the demise of the VU, focusing on Cale and Nico, with brief VU recollections and a photograph of Nico live.

Magazine: Rolling Stone
Article: "1990 Yearbook – June"
(No. 593/594, 13-27 December 1990, New York)
Of note: Brief story and color photograph of the VU at the June 1990 Cartier reunion.

Magazine: Sounds
Article: "Velvets Reform for One Song in Paris – More to Come?"
(30 June 1990, London)
Of note: News item following the Cartier reunion.

Magazine: Spin
Article: "The 25 Greatest Albums of All Time"
(Vol. 5, No. 1, April 1989, New York)
Of note: 1. VU & Nico placed at #18 – "rock's coolest band."
2. **I'm Waiting For The Man** at #70 on their 100 Greatest Singles list (citing a "1967 MGM/Verve" issue – but **Waiting** never came out on 45 in the USA).

Magazine: TV Times
Article: "Underground Travellers in Time"
(26 April 1986, London)
Of note: Preview of 'South Bank Show' TV documentary.

Magazine: Village Voice
Article: "Pop Eye" column
(26 September 1968, New York)
Of note: Preview of Nico's album **The Marble Index**.

Magazine: Village Voice
Article: "Pop Eye – Albums to Avoid" column
(5 December 1968, New York)
Of note: One line dismissal of **The Marble Index**: "Because – despite some impressive arrangements by John Cale – it is this year's most stunning example of the confusion of art with chic."

APPENDICES

Appendix I

The Velvet Underground & Nico
A History of the First Album

Verve V-5008 (mono), March 1966
Side 1: Sunday Morning, I'm Waiting For The Man, Femme Fatale, Venus In Furs, Run Run Run, All Tomorrow's Parties
Side 2: Heroin, There She Goes Again, I'll Be Your Mirror, The Black Angel's Death Song, European Son
The players: Maureen Tucker (Percussion), Lou Reed (Lead Guitar, Ostrich Guitar, Vocal), John Cale (Electric Viola, Piano, Bass Guitar), Sterling Morrison (Rhythm Guitar, Bass Guitar), Nico (Chanteuse)

For an album recorded in four days, mixed (for mono) in another, released by a record company that had no idea whatinhell was going on, and wrapped in a mysterious package that gave scant clue to what lay within, behold! Not only does **The Velvet Underground and Nico** album survive, it thrives! Prepare for an odd, complicated journey. This record, which always makes the top 20 lists (for both the music and the cover), has been through many strange changes...

Sterling Morrison says the LP was recorded and mixed in mono, for mono listening. The 'stereo' is artificially created. So the true mono is a great (and about the only) place to hear the original Velvets as a living, working rock and roll band.

Andy Warhol is credited with producing this album. It says so right on the spine. Sounds/looks fab, but Andy produced this in much the same fashion as the films he was associated with at the time: he arranged finances, places, dates, people, and loosely supervised production. Most of the producing was done by the band themselves, with the important collaboration of Tom Wilson. Tom was a most hip producer (Dylan, Zappa, Animals) – he did the great things with **Venus In Furs**, **All Tomorrow's Parties**, **Sunday Morning**, **I'm Waiting For The Man**, and **Heroin**. (Recording engineer for the record was Norman Dolph, who went on to co-write Reunion's 1974 hit single **Life Is A Rock**.)

Warhol also provided the band with the banana. He had already done the banana as a silkscreen in 1965, and now the band agreed it could be the basis for a fine album cover, so Andy went down to the local record shop to see what sort of designs worked. He came back saying that white stood out the best, and the fewer words the better. Then Andy recalled an ad in 'Life' magazine for bananas, which had shown a banana with the peel halfway peeled down, revealing all the vitamins and nutrients in the fruit. From there came the 'Peel slowly and see' tease of the original cover, one of the greatest album cover designs ever. 'Peel slowly and see'... a pink banana! Irresistible – how many copies have you seen with the peel untouched?! 'Rolling Stone', November 11, 1991, named the cover #10 in their list of top 100 LP covers of all time.

The original issue of the album also carries the disappeared actor on the cover. Originally, the big photograph of the band was framed on top and sides in superimposed light-show fashion by the upper torso of one of the actors from Warhol's 'Chelsea Girls' film.

According to Sterling Morrison, "This guy, Eric Emerson, got busted with about 1000 hits of acid, and was desperate for some money. Seeing how no one asked him about putting his picture on the cover, he asked Verve for a lot of money. Verve got scared and airbrushed it out."

Indeed. But first they slapped big black and white 'Velvet Underground and Nico' stickers over the entire photograph on all the copies they had left in stock, before airbrushing Eric into a hazy light-show blob on all future copies.

The promo push for the record was simple. The band asked Verve to put promo money into tour support rather than pushing the record directly, and the original press kit could be looked on today as elegant in its simplicity, to put the best face on it: there was a single sheet of paper (Verve stationary, with a purple circle around the Verve logo) with this typed announcement:

'BANANAS ARE IN SEASON'

THE VELVET UNDERGROUND & NICO
Produced By ANDY WARHOL
V/V6-5008

There you go. A few copies, for VIPs, came with the front page of the 30 March 1966 'Wall Street Journal', with a banana sticker bordering a story headlined: 'Light Up a Banana: Students Bake Peels To Kick Up Their Heels', about the current fad of smoking banana peels ("a mild high, reports one student, similar to weak marijuana..."). This was an odd way to pitch the LP. "We were horrified at being topical," says Sterling. "We had the entire package ready a year earlier, before any of this had come about, and now it looked as if we were trying to cash in on this."

Now there's no more 'Peel slowly and see.' Hard times have just about eliminated the pink banana from modern society. Almost every current version of the first LP comes with a rather crude printed banana. In the US, the album has gone in and out of print. Verve had a printed banana cover with a gatefold until Polydor bought the Verve/MGM catalog in 1976. In 1981 it joined the low-budget racks with budget-line packaging: no gatefold, and song titles and info printed on the back, with the LP title on the front.

Let's take a quick check of how many ways the Velvets' first record has come out just in the US. I'm not talking collections or separate songs, but as the entire album, **The Velvet Underground & Nico**:

The originals:

1. banana peel/gatefold/Eric Emerson on the back/blue label/mono/Verve Records dist. by MGM
2. banana peel/gatefold/Eric Emerson on the back/blue label/stereo/Verve Records dist. by MGM
3. banana peel/gatefold/Eric Emerson on the back/

yellow promo label/mono/Verve Records dist. by MGM
4. banana peel/gatefold/Eric Emerson on the back/ yellow promo label/stereo/Verve Records dist. by MGM
5. banana peel/gatefold/Eric Emerson on the back/ white promo label/ mono/Verve Records dist. by MGM
6. banana peel/gatefold/Eric Emerson on the back/ white promo label/stereo/Verve Records dist. by MGM

The Emerson-lawsuit-threat stickers:

7. banana peel/gatefold/big black sticker on the back/ blue label/mono/Verve Records dist. by MGM
8. banana peel/gatefold/big black sticker on the back/ blue label/stereo/Verve Records dist. by MGM

The Emerson-lawsuit-threat permanent solution (1st reissue):

9. banana peel/gatefold/airbrushed Emerson/blue label/mono/Verve Records dist. by MGM
10. banana peel/gatefold/airbrushed Emerson/blue label/stereo/Verve Records dist. by MGM

The second reissue (1969):

11. glossy, close-cut banana peel/glossy cover with gatefold/airbrushed Emerson/blue label/stereo/ Verve Records dist. by MGM/Hollywood label address

The third reissue (1971):

12. printed banana/gatefold/airbrushed Emerson/blue label/stereo/Verve Records dist. by MGM

The fourth reissue (1973):

13. printed banana/gatefold/airbrushed Emerson/white label with Verve and MGM lion logos in circles/ stereo/Verve Records dist. by MGM

The fifth reissue (1975):

14. printed banana/gatefold/airbrushed Emerson/black label/stereo/Verve Records dist. by Polydor

The sixth reissue (1978):

15. printed banana/no gatefold/airbrushed Emerson/ black label/"THE VELVET UNDERGROUND & NICO' printed in upper left-hand corner/stereo/ Verve Records dist. by Polydor and PolyGram

The seventh reissue (1980):

16. printed banana/no gatefold/airbrushed Emerson/ black label/"THE VELVET UNDERGROUND & NICO' printed in upper left-hand corner/stereo/ 'Polygram Classics' on label, with address on 55th St./Verve Records dist. by Polydor and PolyGram

The eighth reissue (1985, digitally remastered):

17. printed banana/no gatefold/airbrushed Emerson/ black label/"THE VELVET UNDERGROUND & NICO' printed in upper left-hand corner/'Special Low Price' printed in lower left corner/computer bar coding/new remastering credit/stereo/Verve Records dist. by PolyGram

That's at least 17 different US versions of the record. And I'm sure you can find copies of the '85 reissue stamped in gold with 'Not For Sale' – promo copies that make for, technically, version #18. And say, there's 8-track, cassettes, CD and perhaps reel-to-reel to take into account. At least 23 versions, I'd say. Twenty-three, and we're not even looking at what's written on the runoff groove, which, if it changes, usually means a re-mastering job's been done. (As a rule of thumb in judging mastering jobs just by looking at the record, those that leave very little space near the label are the best. This is a long album – over 45 minutes long – and the masterings that leave lots of room near the label compress the grooves too much and reduce the sonic level.)

Why have the prices for a good copy of the first edition of the album climbed to the $50-250 range? Interest is still high in the band, there were few copies of the record made back then, the sound is different from the 1985 reissue, the white covers were hard to keep clean (few people collected then), and nobody could keep their hands off the banana. Also, the recent deaths of Andy Warhol and Nico have underscored the notion that time is passing, that this album is indeed a classic collaboration between innovators, the likes of which come about rarely. And after all, each original cover is itself a brilliant piece of Pop Art by the master, Andy Warhol.

SOME NOTES ON FOREIGN VERSIONS

The original UK version did not open up, had the back of the US cover as its front (with Emerson, and then without, as did the Canadian versions), and info from the US gatefold on the back. England imported original banana covers and put UK-made records inside them in the 60s. I've also seen the opposite – a British banana cover housing a US-made record; the cover is a gatefold with a printed banana, the label is MGM – with the blue/gold yin-yang wave design from the early 70's, same as the VU's third album came on in the US, except that where the US version is 50-50 blue/gold, this UK one is 2/3rd's blue (off-center yin-yang?) – and reads 'Manufactured in the U.S.A. and Distributed by Polydor Ltd'; the song publishing company is listed as 'Sunbury Music Ltd.,' as opposed to the 'Three-Prong Music' on USA versions of the record; for good measure it also says 'MADE IN U.S.A.' again on the label, which is very odd as MGM never released an edition of the record in the USA.

Mexico put out the first LP in '84, with a different cover showing a late '70s blue Lou blowing smoke, as #30 in the Polydor series 'Anos De Musica Rock'. Unfortunately they put a photograph of the group with Doug Yule on the back cover.

The only people doing the banana any justice these days are the Japanese. The best version of the first album after the US original is an early Japanese issue – real good-looking peel-off banana, gatefold, and great sound. Their current edition features a superb pressing, Japanese/English lyrics (with many humorous mistakes, of course, in the transcription of Lou's street talk. For example, in **I'm Waiting For The Man**, Lou's hilarious 'Pardon me sir, it's farthest from my mind/I'm just looking for a dear dear friend of mine' becomes 'Look on me sir, it swirls through my mind/I'm just looking for a dirty friend of mine'), and a peelable banana. Even if there's no gatefold and it is a rather flimsy plastic banana, the thought was there. The only real flaws in the Japanese editions are: not using the original mono mix, no Eric Emerson, and cover art a generation removed.

The original German version had a different label design and, as in Britain, imported, airbrushed, peelable banana covers from the USA with Verve stickers over the US numbers. The next edition (Verve 2304 163) had a gatefold and printed banana.

In 1979, Italy and Germany issued a version of the LP with no-peel bananas, no gatefold, and only song titles and band members' names on the back.

In 1978, Arista UK made a nice 12" of Lou Reed's **Street Hassle** by popping **I'm Waiting For The Man** and **Venus In Furs** onto the flip. In 1982, Polydor UK made some other tracks from the first LP sound great with a 12" of **Heroin/Venus In Furs/Run Run Run/and I'm Waiting For The Man**. They messed up, though, with a Doug Yule-era photograph on the front.

New Zealand saw the LP issued at first on Verve's blue label, marketed by PolyGram. The cover was similar to the odd UK one, with the back of the US cover on the front, and the newspaper clippings and black and white photographs from inside the US gatefold on the back cover. The reissue (Polydor 2304 163) was similar to the German and Italian versions.

In March of 1985, Verve followed up their **V.U.** release by reissuing the first three LPs as budget $5.98 items. As they couldn't remix the original tapes (the original plan), they used the best copies of the original tapes they could find (from Japan, natch) and remastered them to clean up the sound. Trouble is, with **The Velvet Underground & Nico** album, TOO CLEAN is the result. In general, they boosted the voices and toned down the wild sounds that engulf the original mix. Thus the insane, barrelhouse piano Cale pounds in **All Tomorrow's Parties** is now not as prominent as Nico's vocal. Nor does the screaming viola charge **Black Angel's Death Song** with its original eerie glee – it too has been turned down. The avowed purpose of these reissues was to make them available while making them sound up-to-date. It's a great thing to see them in stores again, but it should be known that these are just not the same records.

The CD says its version of **All Tomorrow's Parties** is 'previously unreleased.' True, but the difference is only in Nico's vocal. On the LP version she double-tracked her vocal – two Nicos singing. The CD version has just one vocal track. It's interesting to hear, but ultimately confirms the power of the original, double vocal version.

Appendix II
CD Song Order
by Jim Flynn Curtin

It may seem sacrilegious to some purists even to suggest changing the song order of the Velvet Underground's records, but with the advent of the compact disk programming feature, it is all too tempting, if only as an interesting experiment. And after all, the vinyl long players were originally made with two sides in mind—two beginnings and two endings. By rearranging the song order, the overall continuity and mood flow can be considerably altered to better accommodate the continuous format. Anyone who has ever put together a music tape knows that the power of each song is greatly influenced by the songs immediately preceding and immediately following.

The Velvet Underground & Nico

The CD version is a remix, vastly different to the album and extremely inferior to it. The problem lies in the mix itself, so there's no correcting this with tone controls. Why the powers that be would take a classic album that has stood the test of time and screw around with it like this is beyond comprehension.

For starters, the vocals have been brought way out front and brightened for audio clarity. The thing is, Lou's voice sounds *better* at the same level as the instruments and not as an over-riding vocal. Who wants to hear every little breath and vocal nuance on a VU recording? More importantly, the raw power of the music has been stripped clean. The trademark thumping drums are washed out throughout the entire CD and now sound tinny and obnoxious. The piano on **I'm Waiting for the Man** has been significantly diminished and mixed into inaudibility during the dissonant ending. **Run Run Run** is similarly destroyed, the drums now sounding like kitchen pots and pans and the staccato lead guitar mixed way back, nullifying its force. The same goes for the viola lead on **Venus in Furs**. Similar toning-down ruins every track, the worst case being **Heroin** – the drums have virtually disappeared, Lou's vocals are way up front, and Cale's viola sits on top of the resultant mess like an unintended feedback tone – even the break, where everything goes nuts, has been cleaned up as well – when the whole point to it was the chaos!

It is a painful task to sit through this CD abomination. If this version had come out first, the VU legend would be considerably different today. The best thing that can be said about this release is that it leads one to treasure the vinyl album even more.

Order: Rather than recommend a new song order, I'd suggest VU fans would do best just to ignore this CD.

White Light/ White Heat

This CD is terrific as an alternate version, loaded with tonal snap. It's different to the album in that the sonic tones are clearer and the instrument separation sharper. There are all kinds of sounds here which are not discernible on the album. Of particular note is **Lady Godiva's Operation**, with its heightened atmosphere of menace; all those weird noises at the end are finally audible—the whispers, groans and moaning come across like a merry-go-round in an insane asylum. **Sister Ray** is likewise great, with the whining guitars, up-front vocals, and piercing organ riffs; the mid-song break where Lou begins his rap starts quieter than on the album and then increases in volume to a kick-ass power punch. The only thing that suffers somewhat is Moe's drumming, but the loss here is not as great as on **The VU & Nico** because all the other instruments are so powerful.

Order: This is such a potent CD that any song order works well, but the following one really hits home: I Heard Her Call My Name; The Gift; White Light/ White Heat; Sister Ray; Lady Godiva's Operation; Here She Comes Now

CD Program: 5-2-1-6-3-4

Another View

When rearranged, this is one of the best VU recordings for pure Velvets feel. It's a perfect bridge over the enormous gap between **White Light** and the third album: it includes Cale songs that could be out-takes from **White Light** and some post-Cale tunes that would have sounded at home on the third lp.

Order: We're Gonna Have a Real Good Time Together; Hey Mr Rain (I); Hey Mr Rain (II); Guess I'm Falling in Love; Ferryboat Bill; I'm Gonna Move Right In; Coney Island Steeplechase; Ride into the Sun; Rock & Roll

CD Program: 1-3-7-6-8-2-5-4-9

The Velvet Underground

Of the original VU studio recordings, this one translates most easily to CD. Although it's one of those classic albums we're not supposed to mess with, a shift of two tracks does make for a more cohesive flow on CD. **I'm Set Free** is the perfect follow-up to **Pale Blue Eyes** and a more logical predecessor to **The Murder Mystery** as it then sets the mysterious tone that climaxes in the latter. **Story of My Life** makes more sense coming nearer the end, and makes a great coupling with **Afterhours**.

Order: Candy Says; What Goes On; Some Kinda Love; Jesus; Beginning to See the Light; Pale Blue Eyes; I'm Set Free; The Murder Mystery; That's the Story of My Life; Afterhours.

CD Program: 1-2-3-5-6-4-7-9-8-10

V.U.

This too moves up from great to classic status when the songs are arranged in a different playing order.

Order: I Can't Stand It; She's My Best Friend; Lisa Says; Inside Your Heart; Foggy Notion; Andy's Chest; Stephanie Says; One of these Days; Ocean; I'm Sticking with You

CD Program: 1-3-4-7-6-9-2-8-5-10

Live 1969, Volume I

Several arrangements work better than the original CD order, with the listing below being one of the best.

Order: I'm Waiting for the Man; We're Gonna Have a Real Good Time Together; Lisa Says; New Age; Heroin; Femme Fatale; Beginning to See the Light; What Goes On; Rock and Roll; Sweet Jane

CD Program: 1-5-2-7-10-6-9-3-8-4

Live 1969, Volume 2

This also sounds much better rearranged. I don't think anyone would dispute for example that the climactic **Ocean** is not a good choice of song to start off with.

Order: Some Kinda Love; I Can't Stand It; Pale Blue Eyes; Heroin; Over You; White Light/ White Heat; Sweet Bonnie Brown/ It's Just Too Much; Ocean; I'll Be Your Mirror

CD Program: 4-8-2-3-5-7-6-1-9

Live at End Cole Avenue

Although this was a limited edition bootleg, it is of near professional quality and is legal in Italy. The song order on the CD defies all logic and is so random as to take away much of the power from a fine set. Try out this new song order and you'll be amazed at the difference. (N.B. The last three tracks on Disk 2 are NOT by the Velvet Underground.)

Order (Disk 1): I'm Waiting for the Man; Some Kinda Love; What Goes On; Beginning to See the Light; Pale Blue Eyes; Heroin; It's Just Too Much; One of these Days; I'll Be Your Mirror; I'm Set Free; Ocean; Femme Fatale; I'm Sticking with You; Afterhours

CD Program: 1-4-13-6-11-14-2-10-3-7-12-5-9-8

Order (Disk 2): Lisa Says; Sister Ray; Blue Velvet Jam; Rock & Roll

CD Program: 2-1-4-3

Loaded

Loaded takes on a whole new feel when the song order is rearranged. For the most part the CD sounds as good as the vinyl, and is clearer, but the quality varies from song to song so some work better than others. Try this order out and discover the connections as one song ends and another begins, suggesting that the song order as released did indeed diverge from the original plan, as Lou has stated for years. Of particular note is that the ending chorus of **I Found A Reason** is literally identical to that faded in at the beginning of **Head Held High**.

Order: Who Loves the Sun; Sweet Jane; Cool It Down; Lonesome Cowboy Bill; I Found a Reason; Head Held High; Train Round the Bend; New Age; Rock & Roll; Oh! Sweet Nuthin'

CD Program: 1-2-4-7-8-6-9-5-3-10

Live at Max's Kansas City

Max's translates the best of all to compact disc, perhaps because there were no extreme high or low ends to screw around with. And the drumming by Bill Yule sounds more appropriate here, if rather standard, unlike on the album, which seems to highlight his enthusiastic, overly flashy style. We still miss Moe, but the loss is less acute. Changing the song order doesn't affect the overall feel as on some of the other recordings, but it does make for a more crisp, orderly set. And not to worry – the classic dialogue snippets between songs (e.g. "You got a tuinal? Give it to me immediately!") remain intact on CD.

Order: I'm Waiting for the Man; Lonesome Cowboy Bill; Pale Blue Eyes; Beginning to See the Light; Sunday Morning; Sweet Jane; I'll Be Your Mirror; New Age; Femme Fatale; Afterhours

CD Program: 1-3-6-4-7-2-5-8-9-10

The Best of the Velvet Underground

Naturally this is a good CD to experiment with as the original song order is just chronological. Unfortunately, since there are no details of the band's commercial history to go by, what constitutes the 'best' of the VU is totally a matter of opinion; I would guess this selection was compiled by looking at which songs had been covered most often. Any collection which leaves off **Sister Ray** has missed the point entirely. Included are **Lisa Says, Femme Fatale, Stephanie Says**, and **Beginning to See the Light** – all good VU songs, but outclassed by many others left off the CD, including **Venus In Furs** and **Some Kinda Love**. There are lots of alternative playing orders to be found here, but this one flows particularly well.

Order: I Can't Stand It; I'm Waiting for the Man; Lisa Says; What Goes On; White Light/White Heat; Run Run Run; Femme Fatale; Pale Blue Eyes; Heroin; All Tomorrow's Parties; Stephanie Says; Beginning to See the Light; Sweet Jane; Rock & Roll; I'll Be Your Mirror

CD Program: 12-1-13-9-7-3-2-11-4-5-8-10-14-15-6

Songs for Drella

There is little excuse for messing around with the order of a concept piece designed as a whole, but for the adventurous, try out this slightly adjusted version and judge for yourself if it doesn't flow a little smoother. This was the original running order as performed live at the St. Ann's church, except that **Starlight** followed **Images** at that performance.

Order: Small Town; Open House; Style It Takes; Work; Trouble with Classicists; Faces and Names; Starlight; Images; It Wasn't Me; I Believe; Nobody But You; Slip Away (A Warning); A Dream; Forever Changed; Hello It's Me.

CD Program: 1-2-3-4-5-7-6-8-10-11-12-9-13-14-15

APPENDIX III: BOOTLEGS
BY JIM FLYNN CURTIN & M. C. KOSTEK

INTRODUCTION

The Velvet Underground led such a short, tumultuous life that little official music was left in their wake; only four proper studio albums were made by the band themselves, and the last two were made without founding member John Cale. Post-VU releases include two live albums and two collections of studio demos, both compiled with minimal VU participation. The songs on all these recordings are by all accounts far more structured than what went on at the live shows. Label restrictions and lack of commercial clout prohibited the recording of the lengthy tapestries of sound for which the Velvets were initially known. Many of the songs which eventually appeared on the albums existed live in several different versions, and countless improvised concerts, especially during the Cale era, went unrecorded. Cale's spontaneity and Reed's lyrical ad-libbing are legendary, yet very little of this free-form style has ever surfaced, the notable exceptions being **European Son** and the incredibly intense 'Sister Ray' from **White Light/White Heat**.

Such a limited amount of product from a band as influential as the Velvets heightens the role of bootleg recordings in any effort to get to grips with the band and what they were really up to. The following points sum up the situation regarding bootlegs however:

1. There are not many tapes out there to begin with.

2. The originals are growing old and brittle, and what little fidelity they may have had when they were recorded over twenty years ago is now fading.

3. Many of the available boots come from tapes generations away from the original.

4. Special care must be taken to achieve maximum enjoyment from these recordings. It is unrealistic to

expect boots from this era to be of great fidelity. (This by no means implies that the overall production is necessarily inferior – just that this is raw product, non-sterile and often refreshingly different in musical content, if not quality.)

BOOTLEG SOUND CONSIDERATIONS

Due to recorder limitations, the music found on older boots tends to be mid-range dominant, and noise (from both the band and the tape) is often an integral part of the experience. Given their 'unprofessional' sources, these recordings are best considered as a format of their own, requiring special equipment to boost and alter the fidelity. If you play them through standard equipment, expect mostly sub-standard results.

This necessary boost is often omitted during mastering. For one thing it brings out additional noise and other sub-sonic sounds, for which no amount of engineering can compensate. Besides, engineering of any sort is tricky with a mono tape recorded in a dubious audio environment, and requires engineering techniques and priorities completely different to the multi-track stereo format for which the engineer was trained. Thus such processing often creates an artificial undertone to the end product. By the time the noise gates and EQ compensators are piled on, the end mish-mash of sound doesn't much resemble the original, and as a result the extra effort and expense do far more damage than good, and the damage is irreversible. No matter how good the original performance or the play-back equipment, such material quickly leads to 'audio fatigue' and becomes tiring to listen to after just a few tracks. (A good example of this is **The Tribute to Andy & Nico** live bootleg CD). Because it is often difficult to pin-point the problem with such recordings accurately, the artist usually gets the blame for what may have been a great performance.

Usually the best policy is to offer the original sound as it was recorded and let the listener process it, rather than risk ruining the original. As long as the source is a fairly accurate reproduction – a crucial qualification – all the highs and lows present during the recording are there somewhere, even if in miniscule amounts. All one needs is the equipment to retrieve them. A graphic equalizer of 10 or more bands per channel will suffice and is relatively inexpensive. (More than 10 bands allows for further separation, but with most bootleg recordings there is not enough difference in the audio zones to warrant the extra effort. Less than 10 bands may not always be enough to achieve a good mix.)

The Art of the Equalizer

There is an art to using an equalizer, but it can be learned. It's all a matter of relative sound ranges matched to volume in an effort to find the optimum point of realism. Here's how to do it: Begin with all the bands in the neutral position of zero and (important!) a loud volume. (Avoid using the amp's loudness button as this adds noise shadings of its own.) Starting with the first three low-end bands (31.5, 63 and 125 dB), find the combination which best reproduces the bass without sounding muffled. Concentrate on the two inner bands, using the last one (31.5) only to boost the overall gain as much as needed. (Most noise is invariably found in the extreme low- and high-end ranges.) Repeat this process for the treble with the last three high-end bands (4k, 8k and 16k), again using the outer-most (16k) as a gain for the inner two. Find a pitch as bright as possible without overriding the bass. Finally, boost or lower the middle four bands (250dB, 500 dB, 1k, 2k) one at a time in varying combinations until they sound good. As these bands control mid-range, often times they require minimal boosting or may even need reducing. From here it is a matter of fine-tuning all the bands until the mix feels right, always allowing for a few moments between adjustments to get used to the sound. (Remember that no matter what you use to process the sound, all improvements are limited by the original source.)

A good 'remix' takes several minutes, but it can transform a noisy, muffled recording into a good approximation of the band live. Although some noise from the equalizer is bound to leak through, it's more than made up for by the gain in fidelity. (In fact, often times the noise can be used as a subtle shading to the overall sound. As demonstrated on **White Light/White Heat**, noise can be a significant musical factor.)

A word about bootlegs which have already been heavily engineered. These should be heard with all bands of the equalizer at the neutral position, or with the equalizer bypassed completely. It is immediately obvious from their super-sensitivity to EQ boosting which boots have already been toyed with – the slightest audio adjustment is magnified ten-fold as the recordings have already been boosted to max, so bass becomes overly rumbly, and treble excruciatingly piercing. The sound on these boots is pretty much locked in as is.

Bootlegs are for the fan with a good audio imagination who wants to know just what the live legend is all about. If you must have studio-quality sound, avoid the often high cost of the boots and stick to the official recordings.

The Essential Collection

There are so many VU bootlegs, with so many overlapping tracks, it's a confusing task to try to figure out which ones are necessary to complete a thorough collection of VU material. So, for the first time anywhere, here's a complete check-list of the recordings that every VU collector should strive to have. As the boots were originally issued in very limited quantities they can be hard to come by, but all are well worth hunting down. (And for the investor, there is also every indication that these recordings will only continue to increase in value.)

Each of these records contains essential VU gems. They are listed in chronological order, more or less. Authorized releases are marked with an asterisk. All are in LP format except where CD indicates compact disk.

1966
Screen Test: Falling in Love with the Falling Spikes
1966
Down For You Is Up
* The Velvet Underground & Nico
(Verve V-5008, original mono issue, if possible)

1967
* White Light/ White Heat
(Verve 825119-1, 1985 reissue)

1968
Sweet Sister Ray
And So On
* Another View (Verve 829 405-2 CD)
Live '68
The Murder Mystery

1969
A Drug Hit Sally Inside
* The Velvet Underground (mix 1)
  (MGM 2353022, original issue)
* The Velvet Underground (mix 2)
  (Verve 815 454-1, reissue)
Shiny Leather in the Dark
Searchin' For My Mainline
Orange Disaster
* 1969 Live (VOLUME 1 & 2) (CD)
  (Mercury 834 823-2 & 834 824-2, CD reissues)
* V.U. (CD) (Verve 823 721-2 CD)

1970
* Loaded (Cotillion SD 9034, original issue)
Praise Ye The Lord
* Live At Max's Kansas City (CD)
  (Cotillion 9500-2, CD reissue)
Everything You've Ever Heard About...
  The Velvet Underground

Post-VU
* Songs For Drella (1989)
  (Sire 26140-1 LP or 26205-2 CD)
Paris 1990

Essential Bootlegs Data

Screen Test: Falling In Love With The Falling Spikes
Release date: 1985 (UK?)
Catalog #: DOM 001 (Shining Star Records, LP)
Songs: 1 – 'Music Factory' interview excerpt/soundtrack excerpt from 'Hedy' (13:40). 2 – 'Music Factory' excerpt (:41). 3 – 'Music Factory' excerpt (:26). 4 – Oh! Sweet Nuthin' (7:00). 5 – soundtrack excerpt from 'Women In Revolt' (1:02). 6 – soundtrack excerpt from 'The Chelsea Girls' (2:31). 7 – 'Vamp' (3:36). 8 – 'Music Factory' excerpt (2:45).
Musicians: 1-3 – Tom Wilson, Cale, Reed. 4,7 – Morrison, Reed, Tucker, D. Yule. 5 – J. Curtis, C. Darling, H. Woodlawn. 6 – Cale and/or Reed. 8 – Cale.
Sources: 1 – MGM 'Music Factory' promo LP, 1968/soundtrack recorded November 1965. 2,3 – 'Music Factory.' 4 – audience recording: live Second Fret, Philadelphia PA, May 1970. 5 – soundtrack recorded 1968. 6 – soundtrack recorded summer 1968. 7 – audience recording: live Woodrose Ballroom, Springfield MA, 17 April 1970. 8 – 'Music Factory.'
Sound quality: Fair
Cover: Original cover is blue, black and white, picturing a heart silouette within a body that looks like a blow-up of one of Warhol's 'Flowers.'
Of note: Reissued in 1987, with slightly different song and running order, in a 12"x12" ziploc baggie, with one sided 12"x12" cover – a black-ink-on-red-cardboard xerox of the original cover with a photograph from the back of the **White Light** LP superimposed. 'Andy Warhol' was stamped in green ink on the inner sleeve in the same lettering as on the first LP. Two postcard-size pieces of red xeroxed cardboard are also included; one shows 'The Velvet Underground' section of the back of the original cover. The other card is a copy of Warhol's four panels depicting Jackie Kennedy Onassis.

Review: This record marks the beginning of VU recorded history, even though most of it is just John and Lou. It's a great, weird compilation of sounds: mostly abstract instrumentals and snippets of dialogue from Warhol films.

Side 1 opens with a brief statement by Tom Wilson about the validity of buying a 'rock record,' and this segues into the soundtrack to 'Hedy,' exceptionally recorded considering that the source is itself a poorly-recorded 16mm soundtrack. Priceless Warholian 'camp' dialogue abounds throughout this thirteen-minute track and meshes perfectly with the musical grunts and groans provided by Lou and John. Side two opens with more of the Wilson interview and then moves unexpectedly into a 1970 live version of 'Oh! Sweet Nuthin'' which somehow fits with the tone of the LP. Next is one minute of hysterical dialogue brilliantly spliced from 1968's 'Women In Revolt,' with the P.I.G.s (Politically Motivated Girls) discussing their man-hating ways. A snappy instrumental track from Lou and/or John from 'The Chelsea Girls' follows, and leads into a short, untitled instrumental live piece from 1970. The record closes with a snippet of interview with John who discusses music as it affects weather!

The quality of the soundtrack cuts and the intimate notes on the cover indicate that the record was put together by a fan in the inner circle of the Warhol/Velvets crowd.

1966
Release date: 1981 (USA)
Catalog #: 104025 (no label, LP)
Songs: 1 – Melody Laughter (?) (27:23). 2 – The Nothing Song (?) (29:34).
Musicians: Cale, Morrison, Nico, Reed, Tucker
Sources: Good audience recording on a mono tape deck: E.P.I. performance at Valleydale Ballroom, Columbus, Ohio, 4 November 1966
Sound quality: Good.
Cover: White, with 4 small photographs of a gyrating female

Review: These are two EPI jams that chug along to narcotic, train-like rhythms. They feature superbly organized feedback squalls, unidentified clunks and clanks, classic Cale piano and viola accents, and Nico wailing away. Sometimes her vocals interfere with the hypnotic drone, but at other times she blends with Lou's 'ostrich' guitar and you can't tell which is which! The whole effect resembles the sort of sounds heard in dreams, orchestrated and arranged to an other-worldly melody. The recording is a remarkable document which alone goes a long way in justifying the Velvets' legendary status and supports the view so often made by the band's members that their best sounds never made it to the studio.

Down For You Is Up
Release date: 1986 (Italy)
Catalog #: none (no label, LP)
Songs: 1 – All Tomorrow's Parties (5:15). 2 – I'm Waiting For The Man (3:14). 3 – Venus In Furs (4:46). 4 – The Black Angel's Death Song (4:16). 5 – Heroin (6:53). 6 – Femme Fatale (2:45). 7 – Run Run Run (8:52).
Musicians: Cale, Morrison, Nico, Reed, Tucker
Sources: Audience recording: live Valleydale Ballroom, Columbus Ohio, 4 November 1966
Sound quality: Fair
Cover: B&w blow-up of the 'Velvet Underground' paperback book cover
Of note: Reissued on white vinyl in 1989: Under New Management Records, VU-1
Review: This offers live versions of all the heavy material from the first LP save **European Son**, with the performances nearly identical to those on the studio LP. The technical proficiency is here, but the sincerity needed to make the songs gel seems to be missing, plus the poor sound is not correctible. **Run Run Run** is pretty good, and longer than the studio version, but the only song that compares well to the studio version is **Venus In Furs** – it's darker, heavier, and heightened by cries from one of the dancers. **The Black Angel's Death Song** is a sonic treble-fest, having no bass or drums; it's decidedly different, but it sounds as if there's something's missing.

Throughout this record one gets the impression that the band, for once, is actually trying to be 'cool,' as evidenced by Nico's affected song inroductions and Lou's sardonic attitude; "This song is about copping dope," he intones before **I'm Waiting For The Man**. Perhaps this attitude was provoked by what was probably a puzzled, unappreciative Columbus, Ohio, crowd – a crowd which remains silently stunned at the end of each song.

Sweet Sister Ray
Release date: 1987 (USA)
Catalog #: SR1 (no label, 2 LP)
Songs: 1,2 – Sweet Sister Ray (21:01;18:07). 3,4,5 – Sister Ray (14:53; 10:12; 25:15).
Musicians: 1 – Cale (viola), Morrison (gtr), Reed (gtr), Tucker (bass). 2-4 – Morrison, Reed, Tucker, D. Yule.
Sources: 1 – audience recording: live La Cave Club, Cleveland Ohio, 30 April 1968. 2 – audience recording: live Boston Tea Party, March 1969. 3 – audience recording: live Boston Tea Party, 15 March 1969. 4 – audience recording: live 2nd Fret, Philadelphia, January 1970.
Sound quality: Good
Cover: Bloody red lettering on a black background; below is a grainy b&w photograph of Cale-Morrison-Reed-Tucker c. 1966 on a NYC street.
Of note: Sides 1 and 2 constitute one of the very few live recordings of the VU with Cale.
Review: This is a great record, revolving around the classic **Sister Ray**. It features 40 heavenly minimalist minutes known as **Sweet Sister Ray**, an improvised two-chord Velvets' masterpiece performed as an introduction to **Sister Ray** and named after the character Lou ad-libs in the lyrics. (The story behind the first version is that one of the Cleveland-scene regulars taped the entire show. Lou asked him if he could hear the tape, the guy said 'Sure,' and gave him his original. Lou later returned it, with **Sister Ray** erased.) This lengthy work-out serves as an extended introduction to the versions of **Sister Ray** on the second record of the set. Side 3 has two great cuts of **Sister Ray** both recorded fast (although a turntable

pitch control can compensate). The first is a flip-out version from 1970, and the second, from 1969, is cleverly edited right after that so it sounds almost like the same gig. Both of these can be found elsewhere (**Metal Machine Sound, A Drug Hit Sally Inside**), though not as well reproduced. Side 4 is the great 25 minute 'guitar amp' version that is killer.

As with **1966**, this is essential Velvet Underground that offers a much wider spectrum to their sound. Excellent presentation in material, album jacket and disk labels.

And So On
Release date: 1982 (Australia)
Catalog #: Second-1 (Plastic Inevitable , LP)
Songs: 1 – Guess I'm Falling In Love (4:07). 2 – It's All Right (The Way That You Live) (2:36). 3 – Pale Blue Eyes (6:16). 4 – One Of These Days (4:01). 5 – Radio Ad for 3rd LP (:58). 6 – The Black Angel's Death Song (2:50). 7 – I'm Not Too Sorry (2:13). 8 – Stephanie Says (2:50). 9 – Loop (6:47).
Musicians: 1,8 – Cale, Morrison, Reed, Tucker. 2,7 – Cale, Morrison, Reed. 3,4 – Morrison, Reed, Tucker, Doug Yule. 5 – DJ Bill 'Rosko' Mercer reading. 6 – Cale, Reed. 9 – Cale and perhaps Morrison and/or Reed.
Sources: 1 – soundboard recording: live Gymnasium, NYC April 1967. 2,7 – rough mix acetates of home demo tapes, winter 1966. 3 – audience recording: live La Cave Club, Cleveland Ohio, 2 October 1968. 4 – rough mix acetate of studio demo, September 1968. 5 – MGM promo radio ad, 1969. 6 – audience recording: live Bataclan Club, Paris, 29 January 1972. 8 – rough mix acetate of studio demo, February 1968. 9 – 'Aspen' magazine flexi-disc, 1966.
Sound quality: Good
Cover: Green, brown and white with renderings of photographs of Morrison and Tucker
Of note: 1. #8 is a different mix to the one officially released.
2. Reissued in 1990; some on green vinyl, others purple/multi-color.

Review: This is a good collection of miscellaneous treasures. The best cuts are **Guess I'm Falling In Love** and, from the great 2 Oct 1968 set at La Cave, **Pale Blue Eyes** – the only version of the song that really works: it's faster and longer than the studio version, and the abstract lyrics ad-libbed here seem better suited to the melody. The rare demos **It's All Right** and **I'm Not Too Sorry** have a wizened appeal and it's great to hear **Loop** in its entirety; the radio ad is always fun, if a bit odd in its serious approach. The liner notes are interesting and accurate as well. The only oddball is Cale and Reed's version of **The Black Angel's Death Song**, taken from their 1972 Paris show – it's certainly different, but is sparse to a fault. Overall, the record works well in its song-to-song flow, creating that certain atmosphere found on the better VU recordings.

Live '68
Release date: 1983 (Australia)
Catalog #: LR 101 (Lurid Records, LP)
Songs: 1 – What Goes On (5:30). 2 – Move Right In (2:41). 3 – I Can't Stand It (8:01). 4 – Foggy Notion (10:43). 5 – Heroin (6:30).
Musicians: 1-4 – Morrison, Reed, Tucker, D. Yule. 5 – Cale, Morrison, Reed, Tucker.
Sources: 1,4 – audience recording: live La Cave Club, Cleveland, Ohio, 2 October 1968. 2,3 – audience recording: live La Cave, 4 October 1968. 5 – audience recording: live La Cave, 30 April 1968.
Sound quality: Fair sound
Cover: B&w collage of headshots of the 3rd LP line-up
Of note: 1. Original issue has the song titles on the b&w labels. Second issue has silver and black labels showing only 'V.U.'
2. Reissued in 1990 as **Up-Tight**
Review: This is one of the best boots in terms of both sound and material: every track is vital! **What Goes On** is totally different to all other versions, with an absolutely spastic solo from Lou, in the tradition of his very best work (such as on **I Heard Her Call My Name**). **Move Right In** is a complete-with-vocals rendition of this

elusive tune; **I Can't Stand It** offers more stunning Lou work, while the version of **Foggy Notion** is notable for its shifting rhythms, samba-like styling and extended length. **Heroin** is one of the rare versions with Cale on viola – enough said. Good historical liner notes as well.

The Murder Mystery
Release date: 1991 (Italy)
Catalog #: BRIG 006 (Brigand, LP)
Songs: 1 – Sister Ray/The Murder Mystery (28:16). 2 – I'm Waiting For The Man (9:15). 3 – Venus In Furs (4:00). 4 – That's the Story of My Life (1:57). 5 – What Goes On (5:31).
Musicians: Morrison, Reed, Tucker, D. Yule
Sources: 1-4 – audience recording: live La Cave Club, Cleveland, 23 October 1968. 5 – audience recording: live La Cave Club, 2 October 1968.
Sound quality: Good
Cover: Portraits of the four band members highlighted with airbrushed coloring on a soft grey background
Review: This is the follow-up to **Live '68**, recorded largely in the same month and with the same great sound. **I'm Waiting For The Man** is similar to the **Live 1969** version, but works much better here as the band is in top form – and they remain so for the entire LP. **Venus In Furs** is terrifically understated and menacing, and this is the only post-Cale version available. **That's The Story Of My Life** is proficient, and noteworthy for Moe's slap-happy drumming. **What Goes On** is the same track as on **Live '68**, but it works well here also. Best of all are the twenty-eight minutes of a restrained **Sister Ray**, loaded with atmosphere, which here drifts into the final lines of **The Murder Mystery** (– this is one of only two known live snippets of that song); although the tune never really changes from the **Sister Ray** riff, it's great to hear Lou cross over to the 'Nuns upon the seawall/sick upon the parapet' lines from **Mystery**. Another excellent live VU record.

A Drug Hit Sally Inside/Live 1968
Release date: 1986 (USA)
Catalog #: CS 1017 (Clean Sound , LP)
Songs: 1 – What Goes On (7:20). 2 – White Light/White Heat (7:18). 3 – Ferryboat Bill (3:54). 4 – Jesus (3:25). 5 – Heroin (7:56). 6 – Sister Ray (10:25).
Musicians: Morrison, Reed, Tucker, D. Yule
Sources: Live 'guitar amp' recording made right through Lou's amp, Boston Tea Party, Boston, 15 March 1969
Sound quality: Good
Cover: Picture disc. Photograph on both sides is purple-tinted shot of Reed and Cale playing and Edie Sedgwick dancing at the Psychiatrists Convention, Delmonicos, New York City, 8 January 1966.
Of note: There is reported to be also a regular, black vinyl version of this.
Review: As this was recorded directly from Lou's guitar amplifier, the vocals and bass are near inaudible. So the songs become sonic instrumentals, and the listener should be prepared for an abrasive explosion that MUST be played loud; and do give your ears a few minutes to err... adjust. (At quieter levels, this LP can be damn obnoxious as all you hear is treble.)

What Goes On is performed with super-cool staccato-style riffing from Lou, and proves that the driving force of this song had little to do with Doug Yule's whirling organ frills, inaudible here (which is not to discount his sometimes great playing, as heard on the same song on **Shiny Leather**). **White Light** is the definitive insane version with a two-and-a-half-minute end section where Lou lets loose his manic guitar style. **Ferryboat Bill**, besides being the only known live recording of this song, is totally different to the cute studio track: Lou plays a harmonic at variance with the song's melody, and whilst normally it would be in the background, here it becomes the melody; the frenetic, repetitive playing gives this version far more power than the studio version and reveals why the song came to be in the Velvets' live set. **Jesus** and **Heroin** both suffer from the lack of any audible instrumentation other than guitar. **Sister Ray** can also be found on side 3 of **Sweet Sister Ray**, and is better reproduced, but at a fast speed, there.

Shiny Leather In The Dark
Release date: 1988 (Australia)
Catalog #: Flight 160 (Easy Flyte Records, 2 LP)
Songs: 1 – White Light/White Heat (4:01). 2 – Sweet Jane (5:28). 3 – Over You (2:58). 4 – Foggy Notion (7:00). 5 – 'Pope Ondine'. 6 – soundtrack excerpt from 'The Chelsea Girls' (16:50). 7 – Dialogue (4:35). 8 – I'm Waiting For The Man (5:02). 9 – Run Run Run (8:47). 10 – Pale Blue Eyes (5:54). 11 – What Goes On (11:12). 12 – Heroin (6:40).
Musicians: 1-4, 8-12 – Morrison, Reed, Tucker, D. Yule. 5 – Ondine. 6 – Cale, Reed. 7 – ?
Sources: 1-4 – audience recording: live 2nd Fret, Philadelphia, 2 January 1970. 5-7 – soundtrack except from 'The Chelsea Girls', recorded 1966. 8-12 – audience recording: live Hilltop Festival, New Hampshire, 2 August 1969.
Sound quality: Very good to poor
Cover: Colored print of the oft-seen Yule-holding-bass group photograph
Of note: Reissued in 1990 on colored vinyl.
Review: Most of the songs here are similar to their versions on **Live 1969**, but not as clean, and as with many great VU records, the grittier tone enhances rather than impairs the sound. For afficionados of Lou's between-song patter, it's all over the place on this record, as the 'producer' was the sort of purist who insisted we get every second of sound whether the band was playing or not. The average interval between songs is well over a minute.

White Light features Sterling's guitar much louder than usual and nicely flavored accordingly. There's also some between-song doodling from him which serves as a pleasant introduction to **Over You**. **Foggy Notion** is a slow, boogie version which suddenly speeds up at the end as if the band either got bored or sobered up. The twenty minutes from 'The Chelsea Girls' is very poorly recorded, probably by a fan at a regular screening, and is virtually unlistenable; although the track is unavailable in this length elsewhere, there's not enough semblance of structure or sound quality to make it worthwhile.

The remaining songs are great. Unlike so many other bootlegs, the vocals are way out front with a superb high-tone timbre to allow Lou's reedy voice to be heard in all its glory, and most tracks are well-EQ'd. **I'm Waiting For The Man** is the all-fast version, smooth and tight, unlike most other versons which start slow and speed up toward the end. **Run Run Run** is hectic and intense, and this is the only satisfying live version. Lou was annoyed by a delay to the band's set ("All I can say is it's about time, right?"), and the underlying anger is very evident in his playing, boosting it to a hot level. **Pale Blue Eyes** is bass-heavy and cool that way; Lou sounds really sad and/or depressed. **Heroin** is done as on the first LP, but less inspiring here without Cale to spice things up, though the one-chord organ sustain is a nice touch and the vocals are excellent.

The best cut is **What Goes On**. It's the later organ-heavy version as on **Live 1969**, but with Lou's guitar riff during the first break, and as on **Live 1969** the guitar and organ duel it out for song dominance. These eleven intense minutes are reminiscent of the agitation that fueled **Sister Ray**. (Interestingly this is due in large part to a relentless sustain from Doug Yule on the organ.) The band may have realized the similarity themselves as they give the song a big 'Sister Ray'-style finish, with all the instruments joining the rhythm of the drum beat. (The fact that Yule's playing is percussive here and builds intensity through repetition is too much like John Cale to be coincidental.) This is one of the very best VU live tracks, and, though marred by the soundtrack excerpt, this is one of the best VU bootlegs.

Searchin' For My Mainline/Live, Wild & Unreleased
Release date: 1988 (Spain)
Catalog #: FATLP 2-3-4 (Fatman Records, 3 LP box)
Songs: 1 – Warhol Interview (:54). 2 – Venus In Furs (1:43 excerpt). 3 – Heroin (2:00 excerpt). 4 – Heroin (5:13). 5 – Venus In Furs (3:23). 6 – I'm Waiting For The Man (5:50). 7 – White Light/White Heat (4:04). 8 – Foggy Notion (7:06). 9 – Beginning To See the Light (5:14). 10 – Sister Ray (8:55). 11 – What Goes On (11:12). 12 – Run Run Run (7:31). 13 – Candy Says (3:49). 14 – Oh Jim (1:13). 15 – I Can't Stand It (5:46). 16 – Sister Ray (20:42).

17 – Sweet Jane (5:20). 18 – Over You (2:54). 19 – Intro (2:38) / I'm Waiting For The Man (6:21). 20 – Chelsea Girl (3:01). 21 – Heroin (7:56). 22 – Sister Ray / Leave Me Alone (16:46). 23 – I'm Sticking With You (2:23).

Musicians: 1 – Andy Warhol. 2,3 – Cale, Morrison, Reed, Tucker. 4,5 – Cale, MacLise, Morrison, Tucker. 6-18 – Morrison, Reed, Tucker, D. Yule. 19 – Cale, Morrison. 20 – Nico, Joe Bidewell (gtr). 21,22 – Reed & band. 23 – Tucker with W. Alexander (kbds), G. Nardo (gtr), W. Powers (bass), J. Richman (vcl), J. Wilkins (dms).

Sources: 1-3 – WNET TV, NYC, NY, February 1966. 4,5 – soundtrack recording, E.P.I. film, live Poor Richard's, Chicago, 23 June 1966. 6 – audience recording: live La Cave Club, Cleveland Ohio, 2 October 1968. 7,8 – audience recording: live 2nd Fret, Philadelphia, January 1970. 9,15,16 – audience recording: live Boston Tea Party, Boston, January 1969. 10,17,18 – audience recording: live 2nd Fret, Philadelphia, January 1970. 11,12 – audience recording: live Hilltop Festival, New Hampshire, 2 August 1969. 13 – audience recording: live Boston Tea Party, 13 March 1969. 14 – audience recording: live Woodrose Ballroom, Springfield MA, 17 April 1970. 19 – Arsenal TV Show, TV3, Barcelona: Cale, 1984, Morrison, September 1985. 20 – BBC TV program on the Chelsea Hotel, 1981. 21,22 – audience recording: live Plaza Las Arenas, Barcelona, June 1980. 23 – 1974 Boston studio recording, released officially in 1980 on Moe's 12" **Another View**.

Sound quality: Varies, but overall very good.

Cover: White lettering, black background, and red-treated version of profile shot of the VU with Nico

Of note: 500 made. Some included a two-sided poster of VU and Warhol photographs (some very rare) backed with liner notes. Others included a glossy flyer of the liner notes; others included a copy of the cover.

Review: This is perhaps the best VU bootleg yet made. It comes in a beautiful box with a great, red-tinted high-gloss photograph of the Nico/Cale-era VU (although Cale is present on only three and Nico on only one of the twenty-three tracks included).

Although about half of the tracks can be found elsewhere, here they have all been ingeniously re-equalized and boosted to achieve a very Cale-era feel, reminiscent of the **White Light** LP. The vocals have been brought up-front and increased in treble, exaggerating Lou's nasal quality and bringing out, albeit artificially, that whining tone we all know and love from his early years. Key instrumental pasasages are likewise accented so that the entire set requires minimal tone adjustments. Equalizer bands should be kept close to or on the neutral zone to avoid an over-processed sound.

The Warhol interview is done in his classic deadpan style, on how the Velvets are his new project, "since I really don't believe in painting anymore," destined to appear in "the biggest discotheque in the world." Excerpts from **Venus In Furs** and **Heroin** taken from the same (very rare) WNET program follow, muffled but great to hear. Next come the same two songs taken from the 'E.P.I.' film and superbly cleaned up. All these tracks run together to form a clever whole. **I'm Waiting For The Man** is another version from La Cave, unavailable elsewhere; it's the best of the slow versions as it doesn't speed up towards the end but remains bluesy for the whole run. **White Light** and **Foggy Notion** are both found on **Shiny Leather**, but are cleaner here and re-EQ'd for a much smoother feel. **Beginning To See The Light** is the same track as on the **Tribute To Andy** CD, but here it is recorded perfectly and offers a great idea of what that CD could have sounded like; this is one of the very best performances of this oft-performed VU song. A unique version of **Sister Ray** follows: Spanish-flavored, if you can believe it; after a fast, chaotic beginning, it moves into an improvised piece which sounds like the riff from **Jesus** at fast speed.

The **What Goes On** here is also found on **Shiny Leather**, but here it has been recorded by a heavy-handed engineer who has added all sorts of timbre changes throughout the song. For example, the treble suddenly zooms way up for Lou's guitar solo, virtually wiping out the bass, and then re-adjusts when the solo is over. This trickery is also used to ear-piercing effect during Yule's organ solo, and then the mid-range is boosted for emphasis on the ending rhythm-guitar section. It's a great effect, if a little overdone, and gives a whole different feel to this song, sort of psychedelic VU. **Run Run Run** gets a similar treatment and achieves a manic intensity. **I Can't Stand It** is another great track from the Boston Tea Party defeated on the **Tribute To Andy** CD and resurrected in all its glory here.

Then comes another **Sister Ray**. This, more than any other, sounds like what one would expect from a live version of the **White Light** masterwork. If the recording date were not listed (10 January 1969), one could easily believe it was recorded within days of the studio version and included Cale. The rendition is similar to that found on Side 4 of **Sweet Sister Ray**, but is much more powerful and perverse, especially in the obvious delight Lou takes in reciting the nasty lyrics. **Sweet Jane** and **Over You** are expertly mastered for great quality, and the lengthy introduction to the latter is heightened in volume so we get to hear all of Lou's ever-curious chatter and some interesting musical doodling from Sterling.

The second version of **I'm Waiting For The Man** is Cale on solo piano in 1984, overdubbed by Sterling's guitar, including an improvised introduction, a year later. This introduction and the dubbed track are among the best on the album. This **Waiting** sounds like pure Velvets, though no thanks to Cale, who quickly goes into one of his nuttier one-note improvisations (– he does introduce the song as "how the Velvet Underground would've played it... without me"). Here it is made quite clear that Sterling was a major contributor to the VU sound. He carries this tune with brilliant style and attitude, picking up all the loose ends left from Cale's deliberate sabotage of the song (– John spends most of the song rapping his knuckles on the top of the piano, calling out to Augustus Pinochet). Next up is **Chelsea Girl**, a solo Nico version amazingly remastered to recreate the 1966/67 VU sound; this song features Joe Bidewell, who gives a great Lou-style ostrich/fuzz guitar performance.

The last side is all Lou circa 1980. **Heroin** is interesting if not spectacular – it ends rather abruptly here, and listeners who want to hear what the original performance segued into (an amazing Sister Ray/Twist and Shout/Sweet Jane demonstration of the power and flexibility that can be achieved through repetition of one of Lou's favourite refrains, the musical fifth) are referred to the bootleg **More Bermuda Than Pizza**. The **Sister Ray** included here is appropriate to the tone of this collection as a whole: it's an upbeat, boogie version which chugs along to a decidedly Motown rhythm, which takes control completely for the coda of **Leave Me Alone**. To close the set is Moe's cartooney, roller-rink version of **I'm Sticking With You**. Thanks to a wacky collaboration with Jonathan Richman, this track builds a true lunacy from the subtle psychosis lurking just beneath the cuteness. (As Sterling says, the song's a poker game: it plays its cards very carefully, never revealing itself until the end. If you don't get the drift the first time around, play it a couple more times.)

That makes every song a winner on this quite spectacular album, including no less than three excellent versions of **Sister Ray**, nine tracks unavailable elsewhere, and eleven remastered songs taken from the best of the live VU repertoire. The only flaw is... why were so few released?

Orange Disaster
Release date: 1984 (USA)
Catalog #: CS 1005 (Clean Sound Records, LP)
Songs: 1 – She's My Best Friend (2:46). 2 – Andy's Chest (2:49). 3 – Move Right In (6:30). 4 – A Sheltered Life (take 2) (2:54). 5 – Here She Comes Now (take 1) (2:29). 6 – Here She Comes Now (take 2) (2:26). 7 – Walk and Talk It (1:52). 8 – Heroin (5:20). 9 – Venus In Furs (3:27). 10 – Jesus (5:15). 11 – That's The Story of My Life (1:57).
Musicians: 1-3 – Morrison, Reed, Tucker, D. Yule. 4,5,6 – Cale, Morrison, Reed. 7 – live Max's Kansas City, NYC 26 July 1970. 8,9 – Cale, MacLise, Morrison, Tucker. 10,11 – Morrison, Reed, Tucker, D. Yule.
Sources: 1-3 – rough mix acetates of studio demos, May 1969. 4-6 – rough mix acetates of home demos, winter 1966. 7 – audience recording: rehearsal Max's Kansas City, NYC, 26 July 1970. 8,9 – from ' E.P.I.' film soundtrack: live Poor Richard's, Chicago, 23 June 1966. 10 – audience recording: live La Cave Club, Cleveland Ohio,

2 October 1968. 11 – audience recording: live La Cave, 4 October 1968.
Sound quality: Fair
Cover: B&w 'silver balloon' photograph of Cale, Morrison, Reed, Tucker
Of note: All the demos have mixes different to the officially released versions.
Review: Even though the three demos which open the record are slightly muffled here (as opposed to their incarnations on **VU** and **Another View**, they sound good and have a feel similar to that of the 3rd LP. Of the two versions of **Here She Comes Now** included, one has very different lyrics to the **White Light** version and both are effectively menacing (Sterling says however that this song was written for Nico to sing, and that she did sing it live – more's the pity there's no tape of that). **Walk And Talk It** is an okay cut from the Max's rehearsals. **Heroin** and **Venus**, from the 'E.P.I.' soundtrack, are with the one-shot line-up with Angus MacLise and without Lou (the line-up that cooked up the music to **Sister Ray**). What a different feel there is to these songs! No tempo changes, and Cale's deadpan, dry vocals make for the most sinister versions; "...deader off than dead," he sings at one point in **Heroin**. And notice how he begins the song: "I know just where I'm going" – giving credence to his claim that that was the original line, that Lou changed it to "I *don't* know..." when they were recording the first LP. **Venus** is also strikingly different here, with a different viola lead and off-beat drumming, transforming it into a whole new song seething in gloom. **Jesus**, not usually among the most memorable of Velvets' songs live, is another favorite here – it's infinitely better than the other versions, with drums throughout the entire song, and runs two minutes longer, with a mid-song break similar to that in **I'm Set Free**, where the tempo speeds up and then slows back down for the finish, creating a more suitable atmosphere for the lyrics.

Praise Ye The Lord
Release date: 1988 (USA)
Catalog #: VU 714 (no label, LP)
Songs: 1 – Head Held High (3:11). 2 – I'm Set Free (4:10). 3 – Run Run Run (7:21). 4 – Candy Says (3:51). 5 – That's the Story of My Life (1:54). 6 – Train Round The Bend/ Oh! Sweet Nuthin' (16:01).
Musicians: Morrison, Reed, Tucker, D. Yule.
Sources: All audience tapes. 1,6 – live 2nd Fret, Philadelphia, May 1970. 2,3 – live Boston Tea Party, Boston, 10 January 1969. 4 – live Boston Tea Party, 12 December 1968. 5 – live Boston Tea Party, 13 March 1969.
Sound quality: Good
Cover: B&w photograph of Moe sitting drumming in sunglasses, sweater and coat
Review: Some of these tracks are on the **Tribute to Andy** CD, but all are much better here. Those with drums feature them way up-front and echoing, giving a heavy feel and solid beat. The **Head Held High** here is the only complete live version on record. **I'm Set Free** has the drums even more dominant than on the clean mix of the third LP, and sounds better. **Run Run Run** is competent, but Lou's playing is not quite angry and/or paranoid enough to equal that on the version to be found on **Shiny Leather**. **Candy Says** is the only known version with Lou singing lead – it's clearly out of his vocal range.

Side two is truly triumphant, beginning with a swinging, drum-dominant, crunchy-bam-bam version of **That's The Story of My Life** – perhaps the most satisfying of the many live versions. Then comes the pay-off – nine minutes of a starkly barren **Train Round The Bend**, which directly segues into **Oh! Sweet Nuthin'**. These are the only known live versions of these songs, and both are totally different to the **Loaded** versions. The quiet, unique sadness captured in these tunes just three months before Lou left the band point to his discouragement and impending departure.

This record symbolically marks the end of the bootlegs, the end of the band, and the end of the VU era. True, **Live at Max's** came a few months later, but by that time it was all show and no feeling – Lou's heart just wasn't in it anymore.

Everything You've Ever Heard About...
The Velvet Underground

Release date: 1982 (UK)

Catalog #: VU 333 (VU, 3LP box, 7", booklet)

Songs: 1– Soft Summer Breeze/Canadian Sunset (3:09). 2 – Leave Her For Me (2:13). 3 – So Blue (2:08). 4 – Why Don't You Smile Now (2:28). 5 – The Ostrich (2:27). 6 – Sneaky Pete (2:10). 7 – Cycle Annie (2:20). 8 – I've Got A Tiger In My Tank (2:08). 9 – You're Driving Me Insane (2:20). 10 – Loop (4:26). 11 – 'Index' (4:27). 12 – Noise (1:47). 13 – Some Kinda Love (3:38). 14 – White Light/White Heat (2:44). 15 – Rock & Roll (5:14). 16 – Ocean (5:09). 17 – Temptation Inside Your Heart (2:29). 18 – I'm Sticking With You (2:25). 19 – Ferryboat Bill (2:10). 20 – Guess I'm Falling In Love (4:07). 21 – Candy Says (4:13). 22 – Some Kinda Love (10:18). 23 – Cool It Down (3:52). 24 – Who Loves The Sun (2:51). 25 – 'I'm Free' (?) (1:57). 26 – I Found a Reason (4:47). 27 – Walk and Talk It (1:52). 28 – Head Held High (4:55). 29 – I'm Set Free (5:05). 30 – I'm Not Sayin' (2:49). 31 – The Last Mile (2:23)

Musicians: 1 – unknown studio musicians. 2,3 – The Shades. 4 – The All-Night Workers. 5-9 – Reed with unknown Pickwick studio musicians. 10 – Cale (perhaps with Reed, Morrison). 11 – Nico, Reed. 12 – Cale, Morrison, Reed, Tucker. 13 – Morrison, Reed, Tucker, Doug Yule. 14 – Cale, Morrison, Reed, Tucker. 15,16 – Morrison, Reed, Tucker, D. Yule. 17 – Cale, Morrison, Reed, Tucker. 18,19 – Morrison, Reed, Tucker, D. Yule. 20 – Cale, Morrison, Reed, Tucker. 21-29 – Morrison, Reed, B. Yule, D. Yule. 30,31 – Nico, Jimmy Page, unknown studio musicians.

Sources: 1 – Juke One Stopper 45 (#JB-2013) by the Carol Lou Trio, ca. early 1970s. 2, 3 – Jades 45, 1957. 4 – All-Night Workers 45, 1965. 5-9 – Pickwick tracks, 1964-65. 10 – 'Aspen' flexi-disc, 1966. 11 – 'Index' book flexi-disc, 1967. 12 – 'East Village Other' LP excerpt, 1966. 13 – version from Val Valentin mix of the third LP, 1969. 14 – mono 45 mix, 1966. 15,19 – rough mix acetates of studio demos, June 1969. 16,18 – rough mix acetates of studio demos, May 1969. 17 – rough mix acetate of studio demo, February 1968. 20 – soundboard recording: live The Gymnasium, NYC, April 1968. 21,22,24,29 – audience recording: live Max's Kansas City, NYC, 27 July 1970. 30,31 – Nico 45, 1965.

Sound quality: Good, overall, with the third LP being lo-fi

Cover: Black box, with either peelable or silkscreened banana (some curving the opposite way to the Warhol original)

Of note: 1. Track 1 is included here because one side of the 45 is 'Afterhours' with Lou Reed credited as the writer. However, all known copies of the 45 have the labels on the wrong side, and so it's the flip-side's medley that appears here. In any case, the version of 'Afterhours' on the 45 is not Reed's, but rather the standard. Reed was mistakenly credited as being the writer.

2. Tracks 30 and 31 came only in the deluxe version of this box in the form of a boot of the original Nico 45 (no PS), along with a xerox booklet of VU articles. The regular version lacked these items.

3. The labels on here have the VU meter design with the needle in the red three years before a similar design was used on **V.U.**

Review: Almost a great box. Two of the three LPs are very well put together, and feature the earliest and last recordings of the Reed line-up. LP #1 is all the pre-VU doo-wop material compiled in perfect order (discounting the wayward curio from the Carol Lou Trio – a nicely ironic opener, intentional or no). It's great to hear the young Lou progress to an increasingly dominant force in the music. After four songs, he takes the vocals for **The Ostrich**, and introduces the Velvets' sound with the appropriately-titled **You're Driving Me Insane**. Enter Cale for the first VU release, **Loop** (slightly truncated here), and voila – Velvet Underground unleashed! **Index**, from the Warhol book, and even **Noise**, fit perfectly here in the context of things.

LP #3 is the other great disc. It has rehearsals and live cuts from Max's not included on the Atlantic release and is altogether more interesting, though with poorer sound. There's a great ten minutes of **Some Kinda Love**, an abstract **Cool It Down** (reminiscent of the live **Train Round The Bend** found on Praise Ye The Lord), a rehearsal of **Walk and Talk It**, an early form of **Oh Jim** in **I'm Free**, Doug attempting to sing **I'm Set Free**, rehearsals (including dialogue) of **I Found a Reason** and **Head Held High**, and a pleasing, spontaneous version of **Who Loves The Sun**.

The main interest in LP #2 is in the demos, but they're all available elsewhere with better sound and running order.

Paris 1990
Release date: 1991 (Germany?)
Catalog #: none (no label, LP)
Songs: 1 – Style It Takes (3:01). 2 – Nobody But You (3:53). 3 – Slip Away (A Warning) (3:43). 4. Forever Changed (4:55). 5 – Hello It's Me (2:56). 6 – Heroin (9:55). 7 – soundcheck excerpts (15:17).
Musicians: 1-5,7 – Cale, Reed. 6 – Cale, Morrison, Reed, Tucker.
Sources: Audience tape: live Cartier Foundation, Jouy-en-Josas, France, 15 June 1990.
Sound quality: Very good
Cover: Chartreuse line drawing of a lily on black background with grey lettering of 'Paris 1990' top and band members bottom. Back cover is chartreuse diamond with Andy Warhol visage; grey lettering lists the songs. Type and graphics are luminous!
Of note: The name 'The Velvet Underground' is not metioned on the cover. The title is a pun on Cale's **Paris 1919** album. The show was recorded in Jouy-En-Josas outside of Paris, not in Paris. A flyer insert includes great black and white photographs and press clippings from 'New Musical Express' and 'What Goes On' reviewing the Cartier reunion.
Review: With the neat title, the discreet omission of the VU name from the cover (in favor of the individuals' names), and the quiet tone of the music, this is one classy package. The jacket and disc label art are unusually professional, and a great excercise in minimal graphics achieving maximum effect. The selections from **Drella** all sound peacefully beautiful, if a bit unfocused, and Lou's call to the sound engineer to turn down the vocal

monitors recalls the best of the VU's schizophhrenic irony. Because of the quieter level of the recording, **Heroin** is very different to the full-force 12" single release – still marvelous, if not as potent. (It's also 22 seconds longer, and sounds right, which means that the 12" may be fast.) The 'Soundcheck' is a run-through of **Drella** snippets – interesting, if unessential.

Altogether this is a very pleasing package which serves as a great memento to a great event (though it might have been appropriate to have included the **Thank You Andy Warhol** flexi-disc from issue #4 of 'What Goes On').

A Complete List of Bootlegs

Pre-Velvet Underground

History of Syracuse Music, Vol. VII • History of Syracuse Music, Vol X/XI • Primitive: Pre-Velvets • 'You're Driving Me Insane'/'Cycle Annie'

Velvet Underground

1966 • A Drug Hit Sally Inside/Live 1968 • A Young Person's Guide To The Velvet Underground • And So On • Bedroom Tape, The • Black Side of the Street, The • 'Booker T' Collection • Collector's Dream • Down For You Is Up • Electric Newspaper: Noise by The Velvet Underground • Everything You've Ever Heard About... The Velvet Underground • Evil Mothers • 'Feed-back' • 'Heroin' • In Concert 69/A Tribute To Andy & Nico • Legend • Live '68 • Live Amsterdam 1971 • Live at End Cole Ave • Live At The Boston Tea Party • Live in Amsterdam 1971 • Metal Machine Sound • More Bermuda Than Pizza • Murder Mystery, The • NYC • Off The Record • Orange Disaster • 'Pale Blue Eyes'/'I Can't Stand It' • Paris 1990 • Paris 29.1.72 • Praise Ye The Lord • 'Ride Into The Sun'/'Beginning To See The Light' • Screen Test: Falling In Love With The Falling Spikes • Searchin' For My Mainline/Live, Wild & Unreleased • Shiny Leather In The Dark • 'Some Kinda Love' • Sweet Sister Ray • Untitled (*1986 release of live recording of Bataclan Club gig, Paris, 29 January 1972*) • Untitled (*1987 release of excerpts from Nov 1966 E.P.I performance and Lou Reed's Metal Machine Music*) • Up-Tight • Velvet Dylan • Velvet Underground – A Symphony of Sound, The • Velvet Underground Etc., The • Velvet Underground, The • Warlocks/Falling Spikes • White Heat • Wild Side Of The Street, The

Appendix IV
Post-VU Solo Discographies
(Original LP Releases and Videos)

Lou Reed

Recordings

Lou Reed
(LP, May 1972, RCA)
Catalog #: USA: LSP-4701
UK: SF 8281

Transformer
(LP/CD, November 1972, RCA)
Catalog #: USA: LSP-4807 (1986 CD reissue: PCD14807)
UK: LSP-4807 (1986 CD reissue: PD 83806)

Berlin
(LP/CD, USA: July 1973, UK: Sept 1973, RCA)
Catalog #: USA: APL1-0207
UK: RS 1002 (1986 CD reissue: PD 84388)

Rock N Roll Animal
(LP/CD, February 1974, RCA)
Catalog #: USA: APL1-0472 (1986 CD reissue: 3664)
UK: APL1-0472 (1986 CD reissue: PD 83664)

Sally Can't Dance
(LP/CD, USA: August 1974, UK: October 1974, RCA)
Catalog #: USA: APL1-0611
UK: APL1-0611 (1987 CD reissue: PD 80611)

Live
(LP/CD, March 1975, RCA)
Catalog #: USA: APL1-0959
UK: RS 1007 (1987 CD reissue: PD 83752)

Metal Machine Music
(2 LP/Cass./8-track/CD, July 1975 (USA only), RCA)
Catalog #: USA: CPL2-1101
(1990 UK CD reissue: Great Expectations PIP DC 023)

Coney Island Baby
(LP/CD, January 1976, RCA)
Catalog #: USA: APL1-0915 (1988 CD reissue: 0915-2-R)
UK: RS 1035 (1986 CD reissue: PD 83807)

Rock & Roll Heart
(LP, October 1976, Arista)
Catalog #: USA: AL 4100
UK: ARTY 142

Street Hassle
(LP, February 1978, Arista)
Catalog #: USA: AB 4169
UK: SPART 1045

Take No Prisoners
(2 LP, USA: Nov 1978 Arista, UK: March 1979 RCA)
Catalog #: USA: AL 8502
UK: XL 03066(2)

The Bells
(LP, April 1979, Arista)
Catalog #: USA: AB 4229
UK: SPART 1093

Growing Up In Public
(LP, USA: April 1980, UK: May 1980, Arista)
Catalog #: USA: AL 9522
UK: SPART 1131

The Blue Mask
(LP/CD, March 1982, RCA)
Catalog #: USA: AFL1-4221
UK: LP6028 ('90 Euro CD reissue: ND84780)

Legendary Hearts
(LP/CD, March 1983, RCA)
Catalog #: USA: AFL1-4568
UK: LP6071 (1990 CD reissue: PD 89843)

Live In Italy
(2 LP, January 1984, RCA)
Catalog #: UK: PL 89156

New Sensations
(LP/CD, April 1984, RCA)
Cat #: USA: AFL1-4998 (1986 CD reissue: PCD1-4998)
UK: PL 84998 (1986 CD reissue: PD 84998)

Mistrial
(LP/CD, April 1986, RCA)
Catalog #: USA: AFL1-7190
UK: PL 87190

New York
(LP/CD, February 1989, Sire/Warner Bros)
Catalog #: USA: 9 25829
UK: WX 246

Songs For Drella (with John Cale)
(LP/CD, April 1990, Sire/Warner Bros)
Catalog #: USA: 9 26140
UK: WX 345

Magic and Loss
(LP/CD/Cass., February 1992, Warner Bros)
Catalog #: UK: WX435

Video

A Night With Lou Reed
(1984, RCA/Columbia Pictures, 60 min)
Catalog #: USA: VH91090
Europe: 7599 38164-3

Hurricane Irene
(1986, Virgin Music, 60 min)
Catalog #: VVD 232
Of note: Includes Lou Reed preforming **Video Violence**

The Secret Policeman's Third Ball
(1987, Virgin Music, 120 min)
Catalog #: VVD 270
Of note: Lou Reed preforms three songs with assembled company.

Coney Island Baby – Live In Jersey
(January 1988, Vestron Musicvideo, 60 min)
Catalog #: USA: 1213
       Europe: 11213

New York Concert
(March 1990, Sire/Warner Bros, 76:28 min)
Catalog #: CO7822

Songs For Drella (with John Cale)
(April 1990, Sire/Warner Bros, 55 min)
Catalog #: 3-38168

JOHN CALE

Recordings

Vintage Violence
(LP/CD, USA: July 1970 Columbia, UK: Aug 1971 CBS)
Catalog #: USA: CS 1037
       UK: CBS 64256 (1988 CD reissue: Edsel ED230)

Church of Anthrax (with Terry Riley)
(LP, February 1971, USA: Columbia, UK: CBS)
Catalog #: USA: CS 30131
       UK: CBS 64259

The Academy in Peril
(LP/CD, USA: July 1972, UK: Sept. 1972, Reprise)
Catalog #: USA: MS 2079
       UK: K 44212 (1989 CD reissue: Edsel ED 182)

Paris 1919
(LP, USA: March 1973, UK: June 1973, Reprise)
Catalog #: USA: MS 2131
UK: K 44239

Fear
(LP/CD, September 1974, Island)
Catalog #: USA: ILPS 9301
UK: ILPS 9301 (CD reissue: CID 9301)

Slow Dazzle
(LP/CD, April 1975, Island)
Catalog #: USA: ILPS 9317
UK: ILPS 9317 (CD reissue: CID 9317)

Helen of Troy
(LP, November 1975, Island)
Catalog #: UK: ILPS 9459
NL: 89 690 XOT

Guts
(LP, February 1977, Island)
Catalog #: USA: 9459
UK: 9459

Animal Justice
(12" EP/7" 45, August 1977, Illegal)
Catalog #: UK: IL 003

Sabotage Live
(LP/CD, December 1979, SPY/IRS/A&M)
Catalog #: USA: SP 004,1990
(Canada CD reissue: SPY/A&M CD004)

Honi Soit
(LP, March 1981, A&M)
Catalog #: USA: SP-4849
UK: AMLH 64849

Music For A New Society
(LP/CD, July 1982, USA: Ze-Passport, UK: Ze-Island)
Catalog #: USA: PB 6019
UK: ILPS 7019

Carribean Sunset
(LP/CD, January 1984, Ze-Island)
Catalog #: USA: IT 8401
UK: ILPS 7024

Comes Alive
(LP/CD, September 1984, Ze-Island)
Catalog #: USA: IT 8402
       UK ILPS 7026

Artificial Intelligence
(LP/CD, Oct. 1985, USA: PVC, UK: Beggars Banquet)
Catalog #: USA: PVC 8947
       UK BEGA 68

Even Cowgirls Get The Blues
(LP/Cass., USA: 1986 (LP) Private Stock, August 1991 (Cass.) ROIR)
Catalog #: USA: R-1267 (LP)/A-196 (Cass.)

Words For The Dying
(LP/CD, October 1989, Opal/Warner Bros)
Catalog #: 9 26024

Songs For Drella (with Lou Reed)
(LP/CD, April 1990, Sire/Warner Bros)
Catalog #: USA: 9 26140
       UK: WX 345

Wrong Way Up (with Brian Eno)
(LP/CD, November 1990, Opal/Warner Bros)
Catalog #: USA: 9 26421
       UK: 7599-26421

Video

Songs For Drella (with Lou Reed)
(April 1990, Sire/Warner Bros,)
Catalog #: USA and Europe: 3-38168

NICO

Recordings

Chelsea Girl
(LP/CD, USA: Oct. 1967, Verve, UK: August 1971, MGM,)
Catalog #: USA: V6-5032
UK: MGM 2353 025 (1990 CD reissue: 835 209)

The Marble Index
(LP/CD, USA: January 1969, UK: May 1969, Elektra)
Catalog #: USA: EKS-74029
UK: EKS-74029 (1991 CD reissue: 74029)

Desertshore
(LP/CD, December 1970, Reprise)
Catalog #: USA: RS 6424
UK: RSLP 6424
Germany: (1990 CD reissue: Reprise 925 870)

The End
(LP, November 1974, Island)
Catalog #: USA: ILPS 9311
UK: ILPS 9311

Drama of Exile
(LP/CD, July 1981, UK: Aura
Catalog #: AUL 715
Germany: 1987 CD reissue: Line Records LICD 9.00106 0
France: 1990 issue: BUDA 82456-2

Drama of Exile
(LP, 1982, Paris Records (France),
Catalog #: C 3813
Czech 1991 CD reissue: Tom K Records, TK 0002-2311

Of note: has the same cover as the French issue on BUDA Records, but this is Nico's version of the record (BUDA's is the Aura version).

Procession
(12" EP, July 1982, 1/2 Records)
Catalog #: 112

Europe '82 (UK)/**Do Or Die** (USA)
(Cass., September 1982, USA: ROIR, UK: 1/2 Records)
Catalog #: USA: A117
      UK: CASS 2

En Personne En Europe 1983
(Cass., 1983, 1/2 Records (UK))
      Catalog #: Cass 2

Camera Obscura
(LP/CD, August 1985, USA: PVC, UK: Beggars Banquet)
Catalog #: USA: PVC 8938
      UK: BEGA 63 (UK CD reissue 1988)

The Blue Angel
(LP/CD, August 1985, UK: Aura)
      Catalog #: AUL 731

(Live) Heroes
(LP/CD, 1986, USA: Performance)
Catalog #: PERF 385 (clear gold vinyl)
      PERF 385A (b&w cover)

Behind The Iron Curtain
(2 LP/CD, April 1986, UK: DOJO)
Catalog #: LP/CD 027

Live In Tokyo
(LP/CD, 1987, DOJO)
Catalog #: LP/CD 050

The Peel Sessions
(USA: CD, 1991, UK: 12" EP/CD, 1988, Strange Fruit)
Catalog #: UK: SFPS/CD 064
      USA: DE18314-2

Hanging Gardens
(LP/CD, December 1990, Restless)
Catalog #: EM 9349

Video

La Dolce Vita
(Film: 1960, Video: 1987, Select Video)
Catalog #: 2561

Maureen Tucker

Recordings

Playin' Possum
(LP, 1981, Trash/Rough Trade)
Catalog #: TLP-1001

Another View
(12" EP, 1985, Varulven)
Catalog #: VAR 11

MoeJadKateBarry
(12" EP, June 1987, 50,000,000,000,000,000,000 WATTS Records)
Catalog #: MOE 1

Life In Exile After Abdication
(LP/CD, March 1989, 50,000,000,000,000,000,000 WATTS Records)
Catalog #: MOE 7

I Spent a Week There The Other Night
(LP/CD, October 1991, New Rose (France))
Catalog #: ROSE 273

Doug Yule

Recordings

American Flyer
(LP, 1976, USA: United Artists)
Catalog #: UA-LA650-G

Spirit of a Woman (with American Flyer)
(LP, 1977, USA: United Artists)
Catalog #: UA-LA720-G